The
ENTREPRENEUR

The ENTREPRENEUR

By
James D. Nisbet

Published by
CAPITAL TECHNOLOGY INC.
Charlotte, N.C.

DEDICATION

Dedicated to my children, Jim, Jack, Mary and Holly; to my step-children, Rick and John Hazard and Carol Holtzclaw; and to my brother, Oliver.

ACKNOWLEDGMENT

My thanks to the dozen close friends who read this manuscript and offered advice and constructive criticism. Thanks to Alice Colcock, my sister, who edited the first draft and to Betty Folts, who edited the final manuscript. I am very grateful to Connie Evans, for many years my capable secretary, who typed it and retyped it so many times.

FOREWORD

The Entrepreneur is an engaging business odyssey of one man's accomplishments in corporate America. But — it is also more. For those of us who know North Carolina and who respect the author for his contributions to our local business community, the story goes well beyond to specific phases of the author's business life: Moreover, this book is a documentation of the "South's rise" in industrial expertise during the last quarter century.

After spending some years with one of the nation's greatest corporations, the author brought his knowledge and experience back to his native area. He introduced to Monroe, North Carolina, the opportunities of high-skilled industry. North Carolina did not then possess technological "know-how," but Jim Nisbet was alert to the state's greatest asset—available labor with a strong will to work—and Allvac Metals became one of the first companies to bring diversification of the economy to the Carolinas.

The raw materials for industrial development were here ... land, labor, markets, water, transportation, good government. But it took an "entrepreneur" to pull them all together. Allvac represented an investment of brain power and imagination as well as venture capital, and the rewards were readily apparent.

Perhaps today, as was surely the author's dream, Allvac could have remained a North Carolina company. Indeed, our state actively courts research-oriented industry, and such companies are clearly not strangers to the local capital markets. The Research Triangle of North Carolina, developed within the past 15 years, is an excellent example of present and future use of the South's financial resources and educational expertise. Such is only a glimpse of the possibilities for expansion and development of our area that entrepreneurs such as Jim Nisbet foresaw some thirty years ago.

—Luther H. Hodges, Jr.
Chairman of the Board
North Carolina National Bank

TABLE OF CONTENTS

INTRODUCTION

In June, 1970, I resigned as vice-president of Teledyne and temporarily retired. I learned that idleness is the devil's workshop and started writing this book. The book covers thirty-five years in business and is written in nine parts.

The story is from "inside business" and therefore reveals some inside information. I admit I had a bit of trouble with that point and had to evaluate the boundaries between an individual's right to reveal and a company's right to conceal.

This is primarily a business book and not an autobiography, but since business life is intertwined with personal life, my personal life is thinly threaded through the story.

As an engineer and a scientist at the research labs of General Electric, I thoroughly enjoyed the pursuit of knowledge, and I accomplished some successes and innovations in the development of super alloys, metals that operate red hot and are used in jet engines, and new processes for making them. While at G. E. the opportunity for starting a new business to exploit the new processes commercially began to evolve in my mind and became an obsession with me. I grew restless and itched to see my innovations further developed into a new business. Then when someone my own age was made boss, I couldn't sit still for that. There were already too many layers of management between me and the president of G. E.

I accepted an offer as Director of Research at Cyclops, Inc., a steel company. My employment at Cyclops was an extension of the same technical activity, but a long step forward in reducing the innovations to commercial practice. The experience there also strengthened my determination to strike out on my own and start a new company for this purpose.

After itching for years to be on my own, to be my own boss, to do my own business thing, I finally made the break and started my own company—Allvac Metals. (The name means all-vacuum-melting). It was a massive change from being employed and well paid to being on my own as an entrepreneur. It was a total involvement. My mind was continuously focused on the new business all hours of the day, seven days a week, with total concentration on the endless problems of starting a business. This was my second business career. It was the fullest, most satisfying career and the others seem mild, easy, dull and less important in comparison.

But to be honest with myself I must admit that the greatest pleasure at Allvac was during the period of the first few years, getting it started and making it work. The innovative times in getting the company on its feet later gave way to routine aspects of running it. As the transition from the creation to the routine evolved, I again grew restless and bored. I sold Allvac to a steel company, Vasco Metals, then we quickly merged with a conglomerate, Teledyne.

A picture of the Allvac plant is on the wall opposite my desk where I am writing. I look at the picture with mixed emotions, with pride, with nostalgia, and can't avoid some regrets in having sold it. I sit here with the stark realization that it is gone forever and I'll never again be the boss there, nor a major owner of my company.

Then I was employed again as an officer in a conglomerate, Teledyne, as a group executive over the "materials" companies which Teledyne had rapidly acquired including Allvac Metals, Vasco, and a company called Wah Chang, and other metal processors. The hierarchy of the executive ranks at Teledyne was again an interesting change and quite a contrast with the Allvac business.

During the period in the late 1960's, when Teledyne was growing so fast by acquisitions of other companies, I filtered into the acquisition business and enjoyed that single-handed effort and the challenges of negotiating to buy companies for Teledyne.

Finally, I reflect upon my past experiences, talk about private investing in the vagaries of the stock market, about sponsoring young entrepreneurs, and real estate investing, all in a more leisurely environment of semi-retirement in my declining years.

Margy, my wife, says, "Let's enjoy what we have while we are here even though we deplete our capital." That is fine, but it is hard to figure the rate of depletion so that the money available will come out exactly right at the time of our demise.

It was a great and glorious ride. It was more than that, a business man's whole career. As I looked back on my newly acquired idleness, I realized that I was superannuated from business before my time.

I wondered whether I would change anything. No, businesswise I didn't think, under the same circumstances, I would have acted any differently. There were personal things I'd handle differently ... relationships with people ... allowing Kay to fly too much.

I thought about that day when I signed the papers to merge my company, Allvac Metals, with Vasco and the time when we signed to merge with Teledyne, and I saw my autonomy as a business leader decline.

I thought about that last meeting with Henry Singleton and George Roberts when I could have compromised and accepted a new but placid job and stayed on, frustrated, in a corporate sinecure.

I thought about my part with Steve Yih in that intriguing acquisition of Wah Chang and wondered if I could have influenced things there to alleviate the bad blood, bad blood that festered eight years and now has erupted again.

I wondered how my technical education could have launched me into such a wide variety of business careers.

Part I
TECHNICAL EMPLOYMENT

Chapter One

A JOB AT GENERAL ELECTRIC

That spring morning when it all really began, I had no qualms about the future. The times were not the best economically, but I had youth and spirit and a couple of ideas in my head, and I figured the world was mine to do with as I wished. Well, almost.

It was an exciting morning for seniors in engineering at Clemson College in the spring of 1937 when the recruiting officer from General Electric arrived to interview the graduates. A job offer from G.E. was considered the top prize for an engineer.

G.E. had a long-standing practice of recruiting at all the prominent engineering schools across the country—MIT, Stanford, Michigan, Rice, Georgia Tech and all, so an offer was a highly competitive business. Also, the depression of the 30's lingered on and we knew that G.E. was hiring fewer student engineers than they normally did in better economic times. The professors at Clemson said they would be pleased if only one or two graduates were hired by G.E. that year.

Head of the Engineering Recruiting Office at G.E. was a Mr. Borring. It was said that he had hired more engineering graduates than any other man. I still have a vivid memory of Mr. Borring, a handsome, articulate man. He quickly developed a rapport with the Clemson seniors during his lecture to them that morning. With a broad brush he painted a picture of employment at G.E. He cited opportunities at G.E. in many areas of that great company. Then he emphasized and elaborated on the Student Engineering Program which had been developed over a long period of time. It was a post graduate industry settling-in process leading to careers in engineering, sales or management. If we students had had any doubts before, there were none now that a job with G.E. was the big prize.

I was fascinated with Borring's lecture about the

largest electrical company in the world and a name that enjoyed the top reputation in industry. But I thought it was fruitless to sign up for a personal interview afterwards because G.E. had the reputation of hiring only the top students of academic excellence. I had missed Tau Beta Phi which was the brand of excellence in engineering. A month before I had gotten an appointment to the Naval Air Corps by Senator Jimmy Byrnes of South Carolina. I had passed the rigid physical exam and was all set and enthusiastic about that at the time, but the remote possibility of a G.E. job seemed to be a greater challenge and opportunity for a better career.

I was elated on leaving the lecture when Professor Fernow, the head of mechanical engineering, took me aside and told me to sign up for the interview. He had spoken favorably on my behalf to Borring in an earlier meeting when he reviewed with him the standing of Clemson engineers. This surprised and pleased me, so I signed up for an interview that afternoon. Fernow was the toughest professor at Clemson.

I suppose many of us, both during our formal education and later on, have experienced the profound and lasting influence of a great teacher. Fernow stands out in my mind as such a person. He was a gruff professor, cold, a rigid disciplinarian and a ruthless taskmaster. I was afraid of him, but developed a tremendous respect for him. Once when I passed Professor Fernow on campus and spoke to him with a self-conscious grin on my face, he stopped and gazed at me with a cold stare and asked, "What are you thinking about, Nisbet?"

"Nothing," I said. Then he launched into a strong lecture about the stupidity of students, wasting their time, wandering across campus to and from classes with blank minds when they could use that time for constructive thinking. He walked away saying:

"Everybody is born equal in that each person has allotted to him twenty-four hours a day and I strongly suggest to you, Nisbet, that you start today to utilize your twenty-four hours a day rather than walk aimlessly across campus without a thought in your head and with only that silly grin on your face."

Now, years later, I vividly remember Fernow and that campus admonition. I must get my thinking done before this hour passes and sets me behind.

I thought I was hopelessly lost with Fernow although I worked harder under his stern stick than for any other professor. Then I was completely surprised in my senior year when he called me into his office and said he wanted me to be his lab assistant and I was to start at 3 p.m. that afternoon. Although I continued to be afraid of Fernow, I learned in working closely with him that under his crusty armor he was gentle and almost friendly at times. And now Fernow was my sponsor, recommending me to G.E.

Later, on interview day back in my room where several fellow students were having a bull session I announced that I had a date with the G.E. recruiter and I would stroll down and get the prize job. My friends laughed aloud. One suggested that I change pants because the pair I had on had a hole in the knee and the pockets were frayed. I said my other pair was even worse and off I went with apprehension.

Professor Fernow introduced me to Borring and left the room. Before sitting down I said to Mr. Borring, "I understand you hire only the top students and I'm not the top nor the bottom either." He smiled and told me to have a seat. He said further that I was the last on his list to be interviewed and he had plenty of time to chat. Half an hour later, to my pleased astonishment, I was offered a job at G.E.

Back in my room when I announced this, my friends laughed heartily and didn't believe it because a couple of them had also had interviews earlier and were told they would hear later. The next morning as we were waiting for classes to begin, Fernow came by and congratulated me on getting an offer. My friends were aghast with disbelief. It turned out that I was the only one selected the first day and two others were notified later.

This was completely unexpected and an exhilarating experience. I also learned the importance of a sponsor, Professor Fernow. I have observed many times in the years since that the men who move ahead in industry are the men who stand out and are sponsored by those in high places.

I graduated a couple of months later and spent two

restless weeks at home practicing typing by the touch method. I discussed the G.E. job and the Naval Air Corps appointment with my dad. The decision was already settled in my mind and I'm sure my dad knew it when he said, "Jim, go on to G.E. and the student engineering program. In a year or two, if you still want to go to the Naval Air Corps, you can and you will have a broader engineering education that will be of great value."

I said, "O.K., Dad, that settles it, but I don't have the money to get to Schenectady."

My dad figured since I was graduated I was on my own. I argued that since I was only 20 I still had a year to go. He took me to the bank in Waxhaw, co-signed my 90 day note for $100, and I left for Schenectady, N. Y.

Chapter Two

STUDENT ENGINEER

In the rain on Monday morning, June 21, 1937, at 7:30 a.m. I walked down Erie Boulevard toward the towering lights of the G.E. monogram high above Building #2 in the Schenectady works of G.E. to report for my first day of employment as a student engineer. I wondered how one gets to be president of G.E. I pondered about the competition.

Five hundred others came with Tau Beta Phi keys. Five hundred came last year and five hundred will come next year and the next and the next. What is the mechanism, I wondered, of rising through the ranks?

My first assignment was testing industrial control equipment located on the loft floor of Building 23 on the 3 to 12 p.m. shift. It was hotter than plowing a South Carolina corn field in August. Fortunately, the work was not manual labor or it would have been unbearable. Our brows dripped perspiration on the face of the instruments used for testing contactors, relays and breakers, all assembled in huge control panels.

Few test men had cars at that time so we walked the mile to and from our boarding house. On the way home at midnight we would stop at a White Tower on State Street for a snack of cherry pie and a milk shake. The mornings were free and along with my fellow test men we learned to play golf at the Edison Club, named for the famous inventor, Thomas Edison, who was one of the founders of G.E.

Schenectady was not very attractive. Rooming in that industrial city on noisy State Street was a contrast to my country upbringing. Daily work rapidly grew routine and the realization that I now had to work every day for the rest of my life was a sobering and unpleasant thought. Working on the night shift limited my social life. "Fellow testmen" (as student engineers were called) came from all over the U.S. and some from abroad. Few were married so there was keen competition among us to date the waitresses and secretaries who were our first female acquaintances.

The normal "test" assignment was three months. My first assignment ended in September. I was glad to pack my trunk and leave Schenectady for a motor-generator test in a plant in Fort Wayne, Indiana. Test men were not as plentiful in Fort Wayne, my work was in the day shift, and I joined the G.E. engineering club. I found the midwestern girls pretty, pleasant, wholesome and even passionate, so my social life improved a great deal over the Schenectady stand.

Testing equipment, day in and day out, was an interesting contrast in the learning process with the labs at school. The work experience was coupled with night courses in engineering, sales and business. After a year of this we all considered ourselves smarter than Ph.D.'s from M.I.T.

The three month assignment in Fort Wayne passed quickly even though it did become repetitious during the latter few weeks. I was ready to pick up and move on to conquer another assignment. This time it was "steam-turbines" at Lynn, Massachusetts, near Boston. There I learned about New Englanders, the cold and humid climate of Boston winters.

The giant steam-turbines were too complicated and expensive to be trusted solely to inexperienced test men so G.E. had permanent test men who made careers of testing turbines. Nevertheless, toward the latter part of our assignment, we learned to handle them well under the close eyes of the senior men. While on turbine test I was also assigned to a prominent turbine engineer. He was a tough guy and complained bitterly when the width of the lines I drew on his "steam tables" were too wide. I was more interested in the price of the turbine generator and how many G.E. sold than in the width of his lines.

It was difficult to save any money at 70c an hour. My mother lent me the money to buy my first car—a 1936 Ford convertible. And with that my standing with my peers was enhanced and my social life improved, even with the Catholic girls.

My three months at Lynn ended quickly and I was ready to move on because I didn't want to be stuck in the engineering office there. I had learned to enjoy the nomad life and a new stand every three months. With my trunk packed, off I went to Bloomfield, N. J., across the Hudson from New York City. The work there was testing air conditioning equipment in a development lab. It was a very pleasant three months with a congenial roommate and girls in New York City, spending more than we earned.

Testing fan blowers and air conditioning systems and trying to develop fans that would blow the most air with the least noise was the substance of the development work at Bloomfield. In another three months this "test" assignment added another industrial product to my knowledge.

I left the busy and buzzing New York area for sleepy and quiet Pittsfield, Massachusetts, where G.E. built electrical transformers. Not little ones like those that hang on power poles outside each house but big ones, some as large as a living room, into which we had to climb and clean— the dirtiest and grimiest job you can ever imagine. To make matters worse I was on the graveyard shift—midnight to 8 a.m.

A business recession had occurred in 1938 and work was slow. I was still paid by the hour at that time and on call if there was work to be done each night. No work, no pay and two to three days per week were about all we worked. Ever since this experience I have been sympathetic towards hourly employees in companies I have managed. It seemed to me that the system was wrong when machines had to be paid for though idle, but the workers were not.

When I went to the Pittsfield assignment, I was told that another man was needed there. I found the opposite was true. I got a few days off and went to Schenectady seeking a transfer to another test where there was enough work to make a living. I found that all of G.E. was in a recession in 1938 and test men were on short hours all over the company.

G.E. evolved a plan to deal with the problem. Thirty percent of all men were offered a three months leave of absence. It was summer time, and being accustomed to summers off while at school and a bit homesick too, I jumped at the chance for this short sabbatical. With a fellow Clemson classmate on test at G.E. I loaded my car and merrily headed south and home for a summer holiday.

In a week or two at home I grew bored and restless. I had no interest at all in my dad's farming activities. My mother contracted with me to paint the house. I hired three young black boys to help and will always remember the paint dripping from their elbows while they sloppily painted the ceilings. This was the last summer spent with my dad. Dad had seen his last child of five finish college and by educating his brood he felt he had accomplished one of his life objectives. He was then about sixty and getting less and less energetic, but more relaxed and philosophical than I'd known him before. He played a lot of solitaire, napped in the afternoon, avidly read the daily paper and complained about that crazy Roosevelt and his destruction of the farmer's freedom.

He no longer fretted as before about the farmer's plight of "too much rain" and "too little rain." His hands trembled so much he had trouble drinking a cup of coffee. I couldn't understand why he couldn't control the trembling hands until now as I approach that age. Neither could I understand why he had lost the great energy and zip he once had. Now I understand. But he was finding a great deal of peace with my mother, who maintained her energy, zip, and enthusiasm and curiosity about everything in sight or mind.

Times certainly change—when I was eleven mother let me drive the car. When I was twelve I drove the school bus. South Carolina didn't require a driver's license then. In that year, the great depression of 1932, the county went broke and I was paid in script. Cotton was 5c a pound, banks failed, and farm labor was paid 50c a day. I always liked to bargain with dad so I sold him my script for 50c on the dollar and let him take the risk for collecting later. It was two years before he did collect. For me this was a long remembered early lesson in finance—discounting risky paper.

Otherwise the great depression of the 30's didn't bother me much. I remember much more vividly during my teens the freedom of the country, the woods, swimming on hot summer days, mother reading aloud "Pilgrim's Progress" by kerosene lamp on winter evenings, ice cream on Saturday night and fresh steak with grits and biscuits for Sunday breakfast. And I'll never forget the taste of the weekly ration of Coca-Cola.

Before the depression my dad was a prosperous farmer. He raised cotton, sheep, corn, wheat, cows, and pigs. He traded horses and mules. In 1923 he bought a second home in Rock Hill, S. C., so his five children could have a proper education at Winthrop College in that town nearby. During the school year we commuted to Rock Hill about twenty miles away early on Monday mornings and hurried back to the country on Fridays. That lasted two years. It was a sacrifice for my dad who had to be alone in the country during the week. It all ended when mother was asked to teach in the expanded country school near home. Dad sold the town house and back we came.

The summer of 1938 ended and I again packed up, picked up my colleague and returned to Schenectady, N. Y., wondering what next?

I was assigned to an outside test of large transmission circuit breakers in a remote corner of the Schenectady plant. Winter was coming and soon most of our time was spent shoveling snow from the tracks used to transport the gear. In December that year I experienced a new low in temperature, -25F. The engineering content was negligible. It was mostly manual and it was damn cold out there. Again I complained to the "test" office, but with care because the recession lingered on and I didn't want short hours or another leave of absence.

Shortly afterward I was offered an assignment at the Thompson labs back in Lynn, Massachusetts, as a metallurgist.

Chapter Three

METALLURGIST

Metallurgist? What's that? According to Webster's it is "A specialist in the science and application of metallurgy—the science and technology of metals." Before accepting this offer I had my last interview with Borring, the man who had hired me at Clemson. Borring told me that during his long experience at G.E. he had observed that engineers frequently made faster progress when they changed fields away from their formal education, from mechanical engineering to electrical or from electrical to chemical or perhaps from mechanical engineering, as was my case, to metallurgy. Any engineering education had basic disciplines applicable to all branches but changing to one other than the degree instilled greater curiosity and an extra effort to catch up and frequently this put one ahead.

Following this discussion I accepted the new offer to be a metallurgical trainee and I was off again to Lynn, Massachusetts, to study and practice a new field—metallurgy.

Another important factor was that the Thompson Lab was involved in the development of brand new metals and alloys for the turbo-supercharger, the forerunner of the gas turbine which later became the engine for jet aircraft.

During the first six months at the Thompson lab I read and studied several dozen books on metallurgy, including all the textbooks that my metallurgy colleagues studied at school. This homework, plus daily experience in the discipline, put me in a competitive position with a few other peers who had graduated in metallurgy—just as Borring had said.

The extra effort proved to be worthwhile. I was rewarded with a permanent job as a metallurgist in the Thompson lab and was assigned to the development of high temperature alloys for turbines . . . a most interesting and challenging job and the basis for a later business career. In reflecting upon this experience I believe it proved that Borring was wise in his counsel. On all my previous assignments at G.E. I was complacent in my confidence as a mechanical engineer—I had a degree. But in metallurgy I was not complacent or even confident and I hustled to learn and I studied hard to compete with metallurgy graduates and after a year or so I did compete and developed a broad education and perspective.

I stayed at the Thompson lab for three summers and three winters. During this time I became very fond of Boston and New England where we sailed and skiied and partied and courted New England girls. This is where I met Janice. Two friends and I owned a 32' sloop. We were pure sailors with no auxiliary engine and operated under rigid rules; as an example, no liquor aboard—a rule that at times inhibited our pleasure.

One Saturday afternoon we were sailing several hundred yards off the coast of Manchester when the wind died completely. The sails flopped about and it looked as though we might be there through the night. An hour before dark Janice and I rowed ashore in the dinghy we always towed. The Massachusetts shore was rocky and deep and we almost swamped several times before docking, but finally we got ashore below a huge mansion on the hill above. We went to the house and told them our plight—becalmed without food or water. They accepted us graciously, invited us in and said they had watched us in our sloop off-shore for two hours. It was cocktail hour for the couple and Janice and I joined them for three strong martinis while their maid fixed us a box of food and drink for the night.

Back aboard the sloop Janice and I opened our box of loot which included a bottle of rum. One of our persnickety owners aboard invoked our rules and declared the rum couldn't be opened. The sails flopped all night and Janice and I kept the late hour watch.

World War II was declared. Gas turbines had to be mass produced. G.E. built a new plant in Fort Wayne, Indiana, and I was asked to be chief metallurgist there. I accepted in ten seconds and a week later was on my way again, back to Fort Wayne. My two colleagues in the Thompson lab who had degrees in metallurgy remained there. I guess the boss figured they would send me off to the wolves in a war plant and save the G.E. metallurgists for better things.

Work was six days a week. A war was going on, and turbines had to be built and shipped to fly in combat in

Europe so the job was confining and difficult. The materials were limiting factors in the operation and the life of the equipment. So pressure on the job was unrelenting, but at the same time a guy had to live, and most of the guys my age had gone to war. I was classified vital to industry and beyond the draft—this suited me fine. I had no interest in fighting abroad.

Through one of the engineers at the plant I met a prominent Fort Wayne family with a very attractive daughter. I was invited to stay with them and later learned that the three older daughters had married young engineers who had, at one time, also enjoyed their hospitality.

We all became close friends, and I was particularly intrigued with the youngest daughter. She was pretty, spoiled, friendly and unfriendly, gay and moody. In six months we were married. Six months later we were divorced, and it took another six months for me to regain my ego.

Kay Gerig worked as a chemist during the summer at the lab in Fort Wayne while she attended Goucher College. She knew my former wife and had attended our wedding. The two girls had been in high school together, where Kay was editor of the school paper and salutatorian of her class.

I needed some extra help with some statistical analysis of material properties and moved Kay into the office to help out. It was a rather dull job plotting reams of data into frequency distribution curves. She did the job accurately with more output than any other girl had. Kay was more than just bright. I'd say she was brilliant. One of her professors at Goucher said she was a cum laude girl and she would have been if she had not dropped out after her junior year. Kay was also attractive physically—striking in appearance with long dark blond hair, big eyes, sort of a Roman nose, with a copious figure and large breasts.

Her attractiveness was distracting when I sat next to her instructing her on the statistical curves she was drawing—her curves were more interesting and I'd lose my technical concentration, and I'm sure she knew it.

This was Kay's second summer at the lab, first as a chemist then as an x-ray technician and now as a technical assistant to me. She made 65c an hour and hadn't received a raise when she came back for her second summer. She spoke to me about that and I gave her a 5c raise. When she was leaving work a few days later she came by my door and said, "Thanks for the nickel," obviously thinking it an insult. I was ready to leave the office and I asked. "May I walk you home?"

She said, "Why not? I'm headed that way anyway."

During the next few weeks before she left for school I was with her all day and dated her at night and was lonesome as hell for her when she left.

Chapter Four
SCIENTIST

The war ended, and American industry began the massive transition from the production of war materials back to the production of civilian materials. The supercharger plant at Fort Wayne was quickly closed down. People were laid off by the hundreds. Engineers explored for jobs outside of G.E. and within. I was nervous about my future for only a few weeks. During the war I met many engineers and most of the metallurgists employed by G.E. Also a few managers and V.P.'s. I published a few technical papers within the company. G.E. had approved a major expansion plan which included a new facility for its research labs and a consolidation of materials and process research. I was invited back to Schenectady to face a new challenge as a research scientist in the field of high temperature alloy development and new processes for producing new metals and alloys—a continuation of my technical work but in research rather than production.

Prior to this time much of the development work in this new field of high temperature metallurgy was done by the special steel companies: Allegheny, Cyclops, Crucible, Carpenter and others. Steel companies at that time were not noted for their research acumen. Yet G.E. was dependent on the improvements in high temperature metals before they could develop efficient and longer life gas turbines to inaugurate the jet engine for commercial jet aircraft. Typical of G.E.'s technical excellence, the company organized a substantial technical expansion, backing it with millions of dollars, to commercialize the wartime jet aircraft which G.E., under British patents, built during the latter part of the war.

I had developed lots of ideas for high temperature alloy research. So, along with dozens of world renowned Ph.D.'s, I undertook my new job as a research scientist at the great G.E. research center with vigor and enthusiasm.

During the five years I was there we organized and I managed a technical group of thirty-five or forty doctors and technicians on the banks of the Mohawk River outside of Schenectady.

About a year before I left Fort Wayne, I had purchased a single engine plane—a Stinson 105, 3 seater. It cruised at 85 M.P.H., so a freight train could pass it against a stiff headwind. But gas rationing during the war didn't apply to private planes and I was mobile to visit home in South Carolina and, more frequently, Goucher College in Baltimore where Kay was in school. Kay and I became engaged and we took a delightful flying trip to tell the families. I picked her up in Baltimore and we flew to South Carolina to tell my folks, then on to Fort Wayne to her folks and back to Baltimore. I flew on to Schenectady alone missing Kay with each passing cloud. Kay's father was a devoted churchman and Sunday school teacher and was lukewarm about his daughter's flying around with this young man, and a divorced young man at that. Kay, too, was a devout Episcopalian. The local rector refused to marry us in his church because I was divorced—a cruel, cruel decision on his part and it came close to queering the marriage. But love prevailed. Kay took a train to Schenectady and we were married by a Methodist minister with Bill Oberly, my best friend, as best man and five housemates as witnesses.

Things went very well for me at the G.E. lab. I even became adjunct Professor at Rensselaer Polytechnical Institute and taught part time high temperature metallurgy to Ph.D. candidates there.

Three of our four children were born in Schenectady: Jim, Jack and Mary. I built my first house on the outskirts of town. Naturally, it had to be the most modern house in town.

Kay adjusted well to the environment. She was a staunch and devout worker in the Episcopalian church which I ignored at that time. Kay's good works were recognized in the community and she was invited to join the Junior League. There are two types in the Junior League: (1) The ones born in it and (2) the ones invited because of their effective community activities. Kay was the latter and served the League with time, energy, and effectiveness as a volunteer in several worthwhile causes in Schenectady and later in the Pittsburgh chapter. These were happy times and we formed many lasting friendships at Schenectady.

The process we developed for producing exotic metals was unique. It did not exist in the special steel industries and those industries had little imagination and interest in investing time and money for commercial exploitations. Along with a few other research labs outside the metals industry, we published many technical papers—a proliferation of papers in the early 1950's proving the case for **vacuum** melting processes. Still the steel industry did not stir.

G.E. approved its first capital $99,000 for the construction of its first vacuum melting pilot plant. Prior to this time, alloys were melted and only partly refined under chemical slags in the contamination of nature's atmosphere. Melting and refining under vacuum eliminated both the oxidation of the atmosphere and the slag.

I worked with the pilot plant group about a year and thought it was moving too slowly. I grew restless with the further research and was determined somehow to commercialize the promising new technology. I had not the slightest doubt that the new process had to be commercialized, because the technical case proved it beyond question in my mind. I was critical of disbelievers and could not understand why the steel industry was so slow and sleepy.

General Electric spends large sums of money on research; their scientists publish many learned papers on a variety of subjects and obtain patents on hundreds of ideas. Poised within all this knowledge are the nuclei for the development of new products and the growth of new businesses. But General Electric did not have a smooth transition structure for accomplishing this. In some instances the development from an idea to a product moved quickly, as when the know-how to make synthetic diamonds was immediately removed from the confines of the research laboratory and gleefully accepted by a department general manager with a profit responsibility. In this case the profit potential glistened. Vacuum melting, the technology I was interested in while at General Electric as the basis for a new business, was not as glamorous nor did it glisten like diamonds. We had to push very hard to scale it up from a ten pound unit to a five hundred pound pilot plant.

During this time I frequently asked Guy Suits, vice president of General Electric research, to send me to a corn field in Ohio, give me some working capital with a little "sweat equity" and I would make vacuum melting into a business.

General Electric's new chairman and chief, Reginald Jones, now recognizes this problem. According to *Forbes* (August, 1972), Jones says he is developing managers with an "entrepreneurial flair" and is providing venture capital in partnership with entrepreneurs who are set free from the company's strings.

Slowly, special steel companies such as Cyclops and Allegheny recognized the value of the vacuum melting process which we had developed to the verge of production at General Electric. We at General Electric were pleased with these signs of interest. I saw it as a new opportunity, finally, to move the technology into the special steel company.

While at the G.E. labs I wrote a ponderous technical book, "Exploratory High Temperature Alloy Research." It was published only within the company and I don't remember getting any raving reviews from my technical colleagues. I also published a few papers in the technical societies, was granted several patents and spoke several times a year in this country and once in London at technical society meetings.

Chapter Five

DIRECTOR OF RESEARCH AND DEVELOPMENT AT CYCLOPS

Thus, my name became fairly well known in the world of metallurgy and opportunities outside of G.E. developed. A long time metallurgy friend, the late Chuck Evans, invited me to Cyclops in Pittsburgh to discuss a new position with them as Director of Research and Development. I spent two days with Chuck, Ed Stockdale, the president; Bill Stewart, executive V.P.; and Frank Garrett, technical V.P. A fine group of gentlemen they were. We evolved a plan to set up for the first time at Cyclops a research lab and to install a Pilot Plant for vacuum melting high temperature alloys. The great character of the Cyclops officers and their sincere appropriation of half a million dollars to start made me realize the time had arrived: Special steel now would enter the innovating necessary for future production of metals.

I accepted the position at Cyclops as Director of Research and Development and moved to a new life at Pittsburgh. Leaving G.E. was not easy after 16 fruitful, satisfying and certainly educational and intellectual years.

We had two boys and one little girl and both Kay and I wanted another girl to match things up. Kay also said, "As long as we are rounding things out you should join the Episcopal Church. You have been procrastinating long enough." Kay had a very effective and influential way about controlling my destiny without being pushy or demanding, but effectively straightforward. She was such a staunch, faithful and devoted Episcopalian that I realized I owed allegiance to her on this subject. She also wanted it so very much for our children. I took the confirmation classes and became a confirmed Episcopalian and learned to enjoy the rituals of the Episcopal Church in contrast with my Presbyterian upbringing. Holly arrived ten months after my confirmation. I never told Holly this before, but she is my delightful Episcopal daughter, much like her mother now at twenty years old, except that she doesn't go to church much, and I have been on a layman's sabbatical for several years. None of our four children have turned out, so far, to be staunch churchmen—perhaps they are intellectually too far out.

My charter at Cyclops was to organize a research laboratory and build several pilot plants for the vacuum melting and processing of metals. General Electric had a 500 pound pilot plant. At Cyclops we built a 2,000 pound unit and backed it with enthusiastic young technical men and for the first time we organized a research laboratory there. In two years that initial plan was accomplished. I think the explosive growth in special metals technology scared the Cyclops management. They seemed to fear their new position of leadership. When things were humming and we were beginning to expand, problems arose at Cyclops. The cost of the aggressive push to maintain leadership was resisted and eventually declined by the Cyclops management because they preferred money in the bank rather than money in innovations.

The steel industry thinks in terms of ancient art—pure research is foreign to it. With fifty-year-old furnaces and rolling mills and with artisans rather than technologists, the industry is slow to innovate.

My earlier thinking was confirmed. I concluded that a new company was necessary to lead the special metals industry in exotic metals. Thus, I left Cyclops.

Part II
ENTREPRENEUR-ALLVAC METALS

Chapter Six

THE SEEDS SPROUT

"There are only a few times in organization life when the individual can wrench his destiny into his own hands—and if he does not fight then, he will make a surrender that will later mock him. But when is that time?" . . . *The Organization Man* . . . *William H. Whyte, Jr.*

In January 1957, when I reached the restless age of forty, I said to myself, "Self, resign from Cyclops, start a new company and call it Allvac Metals."

Following my resignation at 11 a.m., the financial vice president of the company shook hands with me and said, "Nice to have known you, Jim."

In his opinion the probabilities of my failing were inevitable because of impossible financing. For three years I had eaten lunch with the officers of the company.

"Can I stay for one more lunch?" I asked.

Bill Stewart, president of the company, responded immediately in his affable way, "Of course, have lunch with us, Jim."

Usually the lunches at Cyclops' round table were lively with conversation and discussion of problems. My last lunch there was one of silence and sadness.

I left Cyclops with the conviction that the business opportunity in the field of special metals was considerably greater than would ever be realized within the ponderous steel industry.

My strong desire to create a company didn't happen overnight. As far back as college days the idea first appeared in my mind and was set aside but reappeared on a continuing basis during almost twenty years of employment. The idea grew and spread and itched and finally captured me. Now I wondered if I could really stand the pain of working sixteen or eighteen hour days for one or two or perhaps five years. Could I live with the continuous possibility of failure, and if failure occurred, could I stand that pain? In setting up a new business and accepting other people's money I realized that other people's money can take control and the founder can be painfully deposed if he falters. But an entrepreneur can't waste time thinking about the pain of failure. Besides, the die was cast and I couldn't turn back.

The new business I had set out to create involved the application of new processes for the production of special metals. My academic interest in this field goes back to Clemson University, where I finished in mechanical engineering and where my technical curiosity was first aroused. My practical experience, and really my education in metallurgy, was the result of almost twenty years of employment at General Electric and Cyclops.

During those years of early employment I was preoccupied with the technology of metals but I was restless and disappointed in the slow pace that innovations in metallurgy seemed to move from research knowledge to practical applications. It was this attitude that finally led me from the security of employment to the unknown future of an entrepreneur.

The entrepreneur is quite different from the professional manager in many respects. An entrepreneur is a business individual who is self-contained and self-controlled. He likes to cope independently, creatively and diligently with the complex problems found in business risk. The professional manager likes to operate in a climate of security and in a state of conformance with ritual and routine and formality and order and compromise.

During my early employment at General Electric, like all student engineers, I was one of the students; then, after a couple of years, an individual contributor as a metallurgist. In the latter ten years at General Electric and at Cyclops I was in the manager and director category and had thirty to fifty assistants to call on to accomplish the work. Now it was an abrupt change in work style when I was again alone and any work accomplished was directly dependent on my own efforts. To get this new company off the ground required that all functions of the business be initiated by the lonesome founder; it had to be organized with people, it had to be financed with outside money. A plant had to be designed, and a location found. While all these bases had to be covered, Allvac had to have orders.

Following my resignation from Cyclops, I set out on a tour from Pittsburgh to New York and New England and south to North Carolina to recruit managers, to search for investors, to contact potential customers, to line up suppliers of both equipment and raw materials, and finally, to settle on a suitable plant site. I visited many people and talked about my grand plan to organize Allvac Metals Company. With very few exceptions, the prospects I had really banked on fell rapidly by the wayside. In the lonely world of an entrepreneur I felt naked.

Here I was with a wife, four children, a high standard of living, and no salary. All the money I had was committed to a business venture.

*   *   *

My first visit with a prospective investor was with an old metallurgy colleague and a good personal friend—Joe Cameron. Joe had been my assistant during World War II at the General Electric supercharger plant at Fort Wayne where we had worked together developing high temperature super alloys. He was a sound and practical metallurgist from Carnegie Tech. I had speculated with him for several years about starting a business and his realistic counsel had always been constructive. Over a long dinner with him at the University Club in Pittsburgh I told him about my plans. Before the meal ended, Joe gave me a check for $1,000 for one thousand shares in Allvac—the first outside cash for starting Allvac Metals. His confidence was the highlight of my first exploratory tour and buoyed up my spirits for several weeks.

Then I returned to General Electric in Schenectady to test the financial daring as well as the personal confidence of old friends there. Bill Oberly, a prominent young engineer at General Electric and my closest friend and greatest moral support throughout the years, had arranged a dinner for a dozen engineering friends and their wives.

They all subscribed. Oberly bought five thousand shares. He is a notorious procrastinator and I was pleasantly surprised at this expression of confidence.

Then I met with the General Electric scientists. In my section, when I worked at the General Electric research lab, were twenty Ph.D.'s and an equal number of M.S.'s and B.S.'s and technicians. A number of the technicians bought stock but not a single Ph.D. bought a share; not even the brilliant and effervescent Dr. Herb Hollomon who headed metallurgy research.

My first call on a prosective customer was to Austenal, the company that developed the dental alloy, vitallium. Vitallium is a material used in the mouth as a metallic support for dentures, primarily for its resistance to saliva corrosion. A curious metallurgist at the research laboratories of General Electric tested this material at high temperatures and found it superior to any other material known at that time for turbo supercharger blades. Vitallium was modified during World War II and mass produced by the lost wax process for turbo supercharger blades. Toward the latter part of the war it was used in gas turbines when jet engine fighters were first introduced. Since then it has continued to be a prominent metal for Douglas and Boeing jet engines.

I spent several hours with the plant manager, Al Talbot. He boosted my morale by giving me the first order for Allvac—$1200 worth. It was truly an act of great faith and indicative of the encouragement that a few industrialists pass on to the entrepreneur. Not only that, I was retained for $500 a month as a consultant to aid the company in advancing the lost wax casting process by vacuum melting rather than air melting.

Naturally, I was jubilant with the successful first attempt to book an order and I hurried on to my next best prospect.

At Pratt & Whitney in East Hartford, Connecticut, I visited the chief metallurgist and the purchasing agent. I pressed hard for an experimental order but to no avail.

"The process of having new suppliers approved, you know, takes one or two years," they said. How can an entrepreneur wait one or two years for a trial order?

Pratt & Whitney had just opened a new jet engine development plant in Florida, and I was advised to go there. Subsequently we did get orders from them. In fact, for the first five years, Pratt & Whitney, Florida, was the largest Allvac customer.

Pratt & Whitney and General Electric were the world's largest manufacturers of gas turbines. I also visited General Electric at Lynn, Massachusetts. There, I was very disappointed when my old friend with the desk by the window, with whom I had worked for two years, not only refused a trial order but thought I was nutty to undertake such a formidable, and in his opinion, impossible task.

I was very discouraged because I thought metallurgy friends at General Electric and Pratt & Whitney would surely welcome me, the metallurgist in business, with a bundle of orders.

Then I hustled on to a more practical prospect for an order. He was Pat O'Brian, whose company manufactured high temperature testing machines which required high temperature alloys in the structural parts. Pat O'Brian understood my needs because he had started his small company a few years before with little money. I spent the day with him and I got a barter deal. He gave me a $5,000 order for material and I gave him a $5,000 order for two testing machines—the first equipment to set up the Allvac laboratory.

I returned to Pittsburgh with about $25,000 in checks for stock and two orders in my pocket. The next step was to sign on my first assistant.

* * *

I thought I had my first management assistant lined up before leaving Cyclops. He was Pete Rossin, a very smart, aggressive and ambitious man who had worked with me at General Electric for several years. A few months after I joined Cyclops, he left General Electric and came with me there as a competent assistant in charge of the pilot plant division. We got on well together. While at Cyclops I confessed my plan to Pete. He was interested and enthusiastic and immediately said he would like to join me. When I returned to Pittsburgh following the first several weeks on the organizational tour I anxiously called Pete to report on the progress, the checks and orders, and to sign him on as Vice President—first assistant. In the phone conversation Pete did not voice his usual enthusiasm.

Pete had no money. His lovely wife, Ada, had worked to put him through Lehigh and Yale after he left the Air Force following World War II. It was apparent that Ada had little enthusiasm for this great idea. Pete was committed to resign from Cyclops shortly after my resignation and join Allvac Metals.

A few minutes after I called, Pete arrived at my house in a new Buick. Before he even climbed out of that shiny vehicle, I told my wife, Kay, that Ada's will had prevailed. Sure enough, Pete had decided to wait, but he wanted to join later. Salary, security, and country club comfort had temporarily eased his itch to be an entrepreneur. Ten years later, however, Pete observed the successes and forgot the failures of other entrepreneurs, and in the frustration of his restless forties he did, indeed, organize his own company.

A competent and astute partner is a great buoy in the perilous financial waters of a new business, but I lost Pete before we got started. I was still alone.

* * *

Someone once said that entrepreneurs "make things happen." My first month in practice shifted widely and alternated from a success to a failure, from chin-up to chin-down, but I pushed on to make things happen.

My idea was to recruit a Board of Directors with each member representing a major function of the business. Allvac being a technical business, I was anxious to have a prominent "Technician" director. So I drove to M.I.T. at Cambridge to see Professor Nick Grant, who might represent the very important technical director function. Nick was a prominent professor of metallurgy and a scientist in high temperature alloy research. After I spent a long day with him and outlined my plans, he agreed to serve. Nick Grant was also an entrepreneur in his own right. He and another M.I.T. professor had started a commercial high temperature alloy testing laboratory in Cambridge some years before. I wanted to use this lab until we could install a lab at Allvac. That also was arranged. Some years later we bought this testing lab from Grant.

Earlier I had met Harry Dalton—a business catalyst. Harry was vice chairman of American Viscose with offices in Philadelphia. On this northeastern tour I had visions of Harry, the multi-millionaire, subscribing to 50,000 shares. After the company was organized, he did invest $10,000 and was elected to the Allvac Board of Directors as a seasoned "business man," serving beneficially throughout the time that Allvac was an independent company.

Harry Dalton knows a great many prominent people and likes to let that be known. Now I enjoy frequent lunches with Harry at the City Club in Charlotte, and we still have some mutual business interests. Once I thought I could top Harry in name dropping.

I had been to Vasco Steel in Latrobe, Pennsylvania, Arnold Palmer's home town. At that time Palmer and George Roberts, an executive of Vasco, and I were considering an executive jet plane operation. We had cocktails together at the Palmers' home to discuss the matter.

At lunch the following week Harry asked, "Jim, where have your travels taken you lately?"

"Well," I responded eagerly, "I had cocktails with Arnold and Winnie Palmer in Latrobe last week. How about you?"

After a short hesitation Harry said, "I was in New York last week at Chase Manhattan and had lunch with David Rockefeller."

Another very capable business man I was anxious to have as an investor and "entrepreneurial board member" was Hank Rowan. Hank had organized a very successful company in the induction melting business. I wanted him close by for advice in creating a new company, but also because he manufactured the heart of the electrical equipment to be used by Allvac for induction vacuum melting. I spent a day with him at his New Jersey plant and after much discussion he agreed to invest $10,000 and supply the major electrical components.

Hank was one of the most faithful Allvac directors. He understood the business and its problems. He was staunch in his faith and constant in his support throughout the seven years that Allvac existed as an independent company.

He never missed a board meeting. In fact, he would come a day early and thoroughly familiarize himself with the total business. His knowledge of the problems and plans at Allvac during the board meetings was unexcelled. If all company board members were as capable and devoted as Rowan I doubt that we would have "Penn Centrals." Too often I suspect the board members of large and small companies represent the "Peter Principle" of incompetence.

Later on we signed up other functional directors: Charles Connelly, a C.P.A.; Olin Nisbet, the underwriter; Ervin Boyle, an attorney; and finally a grand old gentleman to represent the community, Van Secrest, Sr., of Monroe, where we settled.

* * *

My two brothers and sister and a number of other relatives and friends invested substantial amounts in Allvac. Brother Oliver joined the company and surfaces frequently in the Allvac story.

A cousin, for example, bought 1,000 shares, saying, "I'll invest in anything if the price is only $1 per share."

This was her way of participating in the grand expectation of future profit on one hand or not being terribly concerned on the other hand if the venture failed. Allvac was too risky, however, for my brothers to allow me to invest any of my mother's small inheritance.

My last stop on this first exploratory tour was Interstate Securities in Charlotte, N. C., the only Charlotte based firm that is a member of the New York Stock Exchange. W. Olin Nisbet, Jr., a cousin, started this business during the depression of 1930 and learned by living lean to make it successful in later years. Before visiting with Interstate I sent them a plan for Allvac, and later signed with them as the Underwriter for a public offering to obtain the needed funds over and above the money from my private sales of stock.

An entrepreneur trying to set up his business begins with the conceited idea that he can invest his talent and talent should attract money. I thought a talented individual with a good idea and a record of success as an employee in industry would be able to match his talent and business ideas as "sweat equity" in equal partnership with others putting in the money: one-half "sweat equity," and one-half dollar equity equalling 50/50 ownership.

Investment bankers think that money attracts talent. In the hours of collaboration with my investment banker I was brainwashed to the point of agreeing with them.

So their opinion prevailed and Allvac was launched by my $25,000 and the private sale of 100,000 shares and then a public sale of 200,000 shares by Interstate in North Carolina.

I personally had to buy all my initial stock and received options on 50,000 shares at an escalated price. The underwriters said this procedure was necessary in order to sell stock to outsiders, the format being an expression of the founder's confidence that the company will succeed and the value of the stock rise.

With equity financing at $325,000 cash in the till, land with a building designed, and some equipment leased and other equipment on order for cash, the commercial bankers smiled wide smiles. They repeatedly stated that as the future developed, as orders were filled, inventories and payrolls increased, and more working capital was required, then the working capital funds on short-term loans would be readily available. We would see!

I had planned to launch Allvac Metals successfully with $325,000. I lifted anchor, but I failed to provide for sufficient safety factors. I should have planned for twice as much money and twice as much time before reaching profits. Soon we teetered on the brink of bankruptcy because we had too little time and too little money.

Chapter Seven

SETTLING IN MONROE, NORTH CAROLINA

While exploring for a Cyclops plant site the year before, I had learned about the industrial attributes of North Carolina; it seemed to be an ideal state for a new venture. The availability and cost of power and gas were competitive with other eastern states. Inexperienced steel mill labor might have been considered a liability by some, but I considered it an asset. The processes to be practiced by Allvac were new and it was desirable to train personnel from the beginning rather than to re-train experienced organized labor. Fortunately, North Carolina was well removed from the United Steel Workers.

As I looked into financing along the eastern seaboard, I quickly focused again on North Carolina for a plant site and soon settled Allvac in Monroe, a town of about ten thousand people, twenty-five miles from Charlotte. Local business men invested, some in Allvac Metals and others in the first Allvac building. Van Secrest, Sr., a prominent merchant and farmer, invested in both and became a director.

After several experiences in Monroe I knew we had found the southern town and rural atmosphere we wanted for the plant site. One evening at a welcoming dinner in our honor, Kay was seated next to an able civic leader on the Monroe Industrial Commission. He was a Baptist and a member of the largest church in Monroe. The two other large churches are the Presbyterian (for the Scotch-Irish) and the Methodist. He said to Kay, "Mrs. Nisbet, what is your church affiliation?"

"Episcopalian," Kay responded.

"That's all right," he said. "We'd like you even if you were Roman Catholic."

On another occasion we had arranged a meeting with Mr. Van Secrest and other members of our building committee for 3 p.m. and they didn't show up. I was not particularly conscious of a heavy rain storm, or was it snow, in Monroe about 2:30 that day until I called farmer Van about 4 p.m. to see what his trouble was. He said, "Since it rained this afternoon, I assumed the meeting was off." Farmers don't plow when it rains.

Monroe has changed dramatically in the fifteen years since that time. Then it boasted only one ancient hotel near the railroad station. Nick Grant, our sophisticated M.I.T. professor and director, spent the night there when he attended our first board meeting. I suppose the residual odors lingered on from the thousands of drummers and peddlers who over many years rocked in the lobby chairs, Southern style. Naturally, Dr. Grant preferred that his directorships be centered around the Duquesne Club at Pittsburgh and on Route 128 in Boston, so he didn't attend any more meetings. Monroe has since that time slowly responded to new industry such as Allvac and now has a Holiday Inn and a Quality Court. Route 74 bypass around Monroe had only one restaurant at that time—Juds. Now for four or five miles that road is lot to lot papered with retailers; Colonel Sanders, Hardee's, McDonald's and dozens more.

The community has developed in other ways, too—from one bank to three, with branches, like service stations, on every corner; and from two bi-weekly newspapers to one daily (they also got the urge to merge). But slower to stir have been the city and county governments. They succeeded in raising taxes and built for themselves the only high rise office buildings in the down town—even taller than the old hotel.

Monroe badly needed an airport and I tried to promote that project for a number of years. I entered the race for county commissioner thinking I could promote the project effectively from that office, but I made two fatal mistakes. I ran on the Republican ticket and only one in twenty-five residents of Union County was Republican. Secondly, the airport was my main campaign theme, and I realized my political naivete when my campaign manager told me, "Jim, denounce the airport plan. Ain't five people in the county outside yourself that owns an airplane so you get five votes and lose five hundred."

Later on, we finally did build an airport in Monroe. Dick Dickerson, a large industrial contractor, and I bought four hundred acres of flat farmland four miles out from Monroe, hired an airport architect to design a 4,000-foot landing strip, then sold one hundred acres through the middle of the property to the City of Monroe. The city, with the Federal Aviation Authority, built a very nice airport.

The General Telephone Company bought out the locally owned and managed telephone company and immediately the union organized their labor for the first time. Service deteriorated terribly and the rates galloped upward.

In every town, large and small, a few citizens stand out above others in civic accomplishments. In Monroe, Jake Plyler is one such person. In addition to being a very successful self-made entrepreneur, Jake had done many things for the city. For example, he organized a group of his golfing buddies and spearheaded the building of a local private country club and eighteen-hole golf course which has been an industrial asset to Monroe. The same group built a Holiday Inn Motel that was critically needed at the time.

Finally, Monroe now has a couple of liquor stores and, separately of course, beer and wine are sold in grocery stores—no bars for Baptists yet.

In Monroe and the county around it, we hired young boys at $1 an hour as trainees to melt and mold metal with which they were completely unfamiliar. Their knowledge of metals was limited to nails and hay-bale wire. The eager ones we kept and trained, and the slow ones we let go.

I was driving home one Sunday morning at 2 a.m. after spending eighteen hours finding and fixing leaks in our vacuum melting chamber. I failed to come to a complete stop at a stop sign and was pulled over by two Monroe policemen. One of them had been a slow trainee at Allvac that we had let go two weeks before. With a wide grin on his face and a badge on his shirt he took me to the police station and refused to accept my personal check for the $15 fine.

In contrast, one of the eager trainees that we kept worked weekends in the silent woods of the county making moonshine. The smoke ascending from his still caught the eye of the Fed peering across the landscape through his

41

binoculars and he was arrested. By this time we had a lot invested in him and I stood by him in court as his character witness. He is now a superintendent at Allvac.

Chapter Eight
BIRTH PAINS

I was commuting between Monroe and Pittsburgh before I sold my house there. Often I returned to the family for a weekend after a full and busy week in Monroe, not knowing at that time whether this Allvac Company would even move, much less fly. I'll always remember one particular weekend. It had been a trying week when more and more problems arose and none of the old problems had been solved. I had butterflies in my stomach like never before. Back in Pittsburgh with Kay I recaptured my cool and was determined to continue in spite of storm, pestilence, butterflies, or come what may. "Come what may" soon came. Oliver called:

"Jim, a thunderstorm destroyed the building last night."

I said, "You've got to be kidding. I'll fly down tonight."

There was the half completed Allvac plant in shambles. It looked like a shingle factory in a windstorm. Was this a bad omen? Was Allvac "snake bit"? We cleaned up the debris and started over.

The most important of all my associates at Allvac was my brother Oliver. He was a major in World War II, and I think three years of battles in Europe caused him to mature and grow philosophical beyond his age. He returned to the South Carolina homeplace, married, and founded a business selling fertilizer that required him to work only six months a year. Later his leisure time bore heavy, and his wife, no doubt, pushed him a bit. (She says not.) So he took on other jobs—raising cattle and, to further help fill in the idle six months, ginning cotton. The gin was an ideal fill-in since it was open for business only eight weeks in the fall. Oliver's livelihood consisted of these various endeavors when I told him about my plans to start a new business in the south.

To my surprise, Oliver said he would like to join me.

I reacted initially by saying, "Oliver, you don't know the difference between steel and brass, so how could you talk to metallurgists about superalloys for gas turbines and exotic metals for nuclear reactors?"

He said, "I can learn and I know something about selling and Southern labor."

What really caused me to sign Oliver on, aside from the fact that he was willing to work for three months at no salary, was the statement of a mutual friend:

"Oliver not only knows the value of a dollar in running a business, but he is also a damn good salesman. You'd better seriously consider taking him on."

So I signed him on but only after he agreed to invest. Oliver contributed tremendously to the success of Allvac. At first he was in charge of building the plant, then integrating Allvac with Monroe townsmen, then hiring initial employees, then purchasing, but most importantly, he was vice president of sales. He is a natural salesman—even my mother-in-law liked him. Oliver would follow me two weeks after I had called on a customer to no avail, and after his call the customer would place an order.

I think, after many years, I've figured out his technique: He meets a customer with sincerity and a firm handshake. The customer notices that his hands are calloused for some reason other than manual labor, and the customer remembers. Then he humbles himself to the customer and listens.

With metallurgists, Oliver lowers himself to the ground beneath them and lets them expound. I, on the other hand, expound on my knowledge of metals and my fellow metallurgists become bored and weary of listening. They don't talk, and they don't call me with an order. But they do call Oliver.

The customer talks, Oliver responds with few words and an occasional homey story and learns all about the buyer. He talks in lower and lower tones. Soon the customer is leaning all the way across the desk to be able to hear him. Their heads are six inches apart and Oliver says:

"It's too noisy here. Call your wife and let's have some dinner."

He charms the wife and the next day the buyer calls and places an order. A customer once told me, "Oliver is the greatest natural salesman I have ever met." Every time I'd see Van Secrest for five years after we had settled in Monroe, the conversation was like a broken record. It went like this:

I'd say, "Hello, Van. How are you today?"

"I'm fine, Jim. How is Oliver? I haven't seen him for several weeks. How is he getting along? You are treating him right, aren't you, Jim? Oliver is a fine fellow."

Under my breath I'd say to myself, "Damn it, I don't know how he is, but I've got a fever and can't meet the payroll, and why the hell can't you be sympathetic with me?"

After we settled in Monroe I was introduced to Charles Truesdell, a long-time resident of Charlotte, a graduate of Wharton School of Business, and an experienced financial man.

Truesdell made an investment of $10,000 in stock and we signed him on as treasurer. Charlie was a wealthy man and had not been working for more than a year. I learned later that he liked to work for two years, then be idle for two years.

Charlie was a very competent, although very pessimistic, financial officer. He stayed with Allvac until our maximum deficit of $118,000 confirmed to him his longstanding opinion that the company would go broke. His doubts, coupled with the fact that he was afraid of a manufacturing plant and that I was brutal with Charlie as well as everybody else during those trying times, caused him to resign. Oliver and I bought out his stock. Once I asked Charlie for a cigar. He pulled one from his pocket and handed it to me and asked for a quarter. I said I didn't have a quarter. Charlie snatched the cigar back and returned it to his pocket.

Charlie's fear of manufacturing operations surfaced vividly at times. Our small offices were built adjacent to the 10,000-square-foot manufacturing plant. The door from the middle of the office hall opened into the manufacturing plant, and another to the outside. Our only office girl sat by the outside door.

One afternoon the plant manager burst in and shouted:

"Clear the building! There has been an explosion in the plant!"

The office girl never left her desk without her purse. She bent to retrieve it from the lower drawer and, in doing so, obstructed the exit.

I jumped up in time to see Charlie reach that blocked exit. He jumped six feet over the top of her head and out the door. Two hundred yards down the street he had barely slowed down to look back. He had always thought the plant was unsafe, and after this incident he was convinced it would blow sky high any day. Three months later, saying we would never make it, Charlie left as treasurer. We scouted around and found that Jack Fowler, a shop trainee for a $1.00 an hour, had some bookkeeping experience. He did the job quite adequately under the guidance of Charley Connelly, our C.P.A. Director.

Finally, we had a manufacturing plant, four employees, and five orders to fill. We bought a ton of nickel, a thousand pounds of chromium, and a thousand pounds of cobalt, and a few pounds of other metals in various proportions for high temperature alloys. And then we melted our first heat, an alloy called Waspaloy, a material used for hot blades in gas turbines manufactured by Pratt & Whitney and later used in jet engines for 707's and DC 8's.

The power functioned satisfactorily; the vacuum tank was pumped down after a few hours of patching small leaks. The heat was melted, and ready to be poured. The pouring chain broke and 500 pounds of molten metal became no more than a large puddle on the bottom of the vacuum tank. And Allvac lost three thousand dollars . . . . 1% of its capital on the first day of production. But we took that in our stride—we had to.

I sold my house in Pittsburgh and we moved south to the full life of Allvac. During the first two years of operations Allvac climbed a steep learning curve but deficits mounted. The directors became discouraged. Two officers resigned and left, and a third, Oliver, resigned but was persuaded to stay. Finally, the stock brokers and the public grew weary of waiting for their expectations to be fulfilled and the price of Allvac shares fell from the high of $1.75 to $.80 per share, which measured their disappointments.

Allvac was not very busy filling orders. Rather, we were busy training farm boys to run a metal mill during the long lag between sample manufacture and customer approval. Tommy Marsh, one of the first local Union County farm boys hired, came to me in the fall of this first year and asked for two days off. I asked why, because he was an important trainee.

He said, "Well, I planted a crop again this spring because I was not at all sure Allvac would still be here in the fall, and I need time off to harvest it."

We had always planned to produce magnets as a second major product. Permanent magnets had a large market in consumer products whereas high temperature alloys at that time were oriented to defense business.

The magnet business also took time to enter, but with it and the growing production of high temperature alloys, business volume was increasing. We were broke but had a successful private placement of $70,000 in convertible debentures. (I again borrowed money on personal notes and subscribed $15,000.) We also borrowed $100,000 from the North Carolina Development Corporation with the aid of the American Bank & Trust Company. But as both businesses were developing and orders were being filled in increasing numbers, deficits continued to mount.

Kay and I spent a weekend in our small lab testing our first batch of loud speaker magnets. We tested about 1,000; of those, 600 failed, but 400 were enough to fill our first order. Oliver took off by car and personally delivered the box to the customer in Chicago and there the customer tested them and rejected every last one. It took a while longer to get them approved.

We finally learned how to make the magnets and properly test them but the yield was atrocious—less than 50% good. I offered a special bonus—a paid holiday on Christmas—for 75% yield. Yield improved dramatically and we added Allvac's first paid holiday. It was later in January that I learned my ingenious farmers found a better way to define yield by throwing the bad magnets into the woods and omitting the bad ones from the count.

During this time (how I'll never know), Oliver persuaded a large forge shop to place an order with us for $50,000 worth of high temperature alloy billets (large bars). We filled it in due time and, by George, the whole batch was rejected outright. We had a pile of scrap and a $50,000 claim and we had no money to pay it. This could have broken Allvac then and there, but the customer was forgiving and allowed us to pay it off six months later.

After this we hired a clean-cut, good-looking, aggressive and smart young N. C. State engineer, John Andrews, to be in charge of quality control. To train John right we had him deliver the first order of bars he had followed through. First he hand polished the bars the 4th of July while his family was at the beach. Then he delivered the load in a pick-up truck to the customer in Cleveland, Ohio. The customer rejected the bars so John hauled them home with an advanced degree in quality control. John was a fast student. A few months later he was made Allvac's first field salesman under Oliver. There, too, John learned fast. The airlines were on strike so Oliver and John took off by car for a week to call on customers in Pennsylvania. The next week he went alone to call on Pratt & Whitney in Hartford. I think customers liked Allvac's naive daring and determination and gave us a better than average chance as a supplier. John advanced on to become sales manager and plant manager and V.P. of Allvac.

The bankers' earlier wide smiles faded to slight smiles—to no smiles—to having just left the office for a few minutes—to being out of town. It is a painful experience to find the great expectation of borrowing money from a bank not confirmed and especially at the very time the money is needed to close a gap between losses and profits.

Bankers in Monroe and Charlotte were very experienced in loaning money on cotton crops subject to the whims of the weather, and on chickens and turkeys subject to the whims of disease, and on automobiles subject to being wrecked. But they had no experience in loaning money on unwhimsical pure metals—metals which cannot be destroyed even by fire and have a worldwide market at the drop of a hat. After the convertible equity financing and borrowing from the North Carolina Business Development Corporation, Allvac's deficit continued to mount and reached $118,000 in eighteen months.

Our efforts to borrow $25,000 from the local bank in order to continue in business were answered with a pleasant but firm no. Like the directors, they lacked faith. But to be fair, bank financing at that time was not a banker's role. The alternative, as the banker suggested, was to borrow to the limit on life insurance to meet the payroll. Oliver was the only other one to join me in this act of faith in the third mile of financing.

*   *   *

We had a small mechanical testing lab, but a very limited chemical lab. At this time chemical labs in steel companies were rows and rows and shelves and shelves of bottles and Bunsen burners to analyze by the so called wet chemical process. Yet also at this time spectroscopy and X-ray were highly developed for analytical work. We therefore built the first lab in history with a spectrograph and X-ray unit and without beakers, bottles and Bunsen burners. We were unable to hire a chemist to run this kind of analytical lab, so we hired a young electrical engineer from N. C. State, Frank Elliott, and didn't tell him he couldn't run a chemical lab without bottles. Frank made it work and work well.

An entrepreneur itches under a board of directors. A board is often a restraining influence; but at times its advice can be very helpful. Being divorced from day to day operations, the board can often bring valuable "outsight" to the company.

After Allvac's first twelve to fourteen months with deficits mounting the directors squirmed, their faith faltered, and they talked about Allvac going broke. Somehow, I never believed I would let that happen. I always believed that Allvac would soon make ends meet. Once, at the end of a board meeting, our legal counsel walked out because Hank Rowan, a staunch director, had berated him and the other directors for their discouraging remarks and expressions of doubt about the ultimate success of the company. Olin Nisbet, our broker director and astute financial thinker, remarked in his deliberate way:

"Jim, I have never seen a company yet that solved its problems with the continuous infusion of money."

He said it in such a way that he made an irrefutable point. So I adjourned the meeting and redoubled my efforts to make Allvac tick. I sold my car and began to ride in the company pickup truck to express to all employees that times were lean and efforts to survive had to be redoubled.

However, redoubling our efforts and fighting for profits demanded still another major investment. We needed a large blooming mill to eliminate the cost and time required to convert our cast ingot to billets on out of state mills. Atlantic Steel placed a suitable used blooming mill on the market at a bargain price, but of course we didn't have the capital and the mood of our board of directors was "no." The economic case for its purchase was beyond doubt so I organized another company, capitalized it for $100,000, and bought the mill on credit. In just three months we had dismantled the mill in Atlanta, reinstalled it at Monroe, and were rolling metal. My late friend, Jack Adamson, accomplished that impossible task with a time bonus incentive. Normally it would have taken one or even two years to remove and reinstall such a massive piece of equipment, including the construction of a new building to house it. The blooming mill in a short time contributed substantially to Allvac's profits and product control. The company set up to purchase it was merged into Allvac Metals a few months after the mill had proved profitable.

Chapter Nine

PROSPERITY

I did drive the officers and employees unmercifully hard, as if to force success by pressure. The result of this pressure was that Oliver resigned for a second time and again I was able to persuade him to stay. I reacted by working longer hours.

A few months later we had finally eliminated losses, and in 1959 the company actually made a profit of $54.60—we were sailing! The public price of the stock firmed up at $1.50 per share.

Then, following a sales trip, Oliver said he could get a huge order if we could make castings twelve feet long. At that time our limit was four feet. It was a tremendous opportunity to book a long-range order.

I said, "Take the order, and we will start delivery next week."

Oliver, of course, wanted to know how we could do it and thought it impossible to do in such a short time. He took the order with tongue in cheek.

We hired a welder and a well digger, dug a hole beside the vacuum chamber twenty feet deep and sank a tank into that hole, connecting it as an integral part to the standard vacuum chamber. We poured the first twelve-foot electrodes the following week. The equipment was engineered a little too fast on the back of an envelope and I forgot to take into account the expansion from the heat. The entire furnace was lifted six inches off the ground and it took another day or two to fix that problem. The electrodes were sold to Allegheny Ludlum at a juicy margin, and Allvac leaped into a very high profit position.

The experience illustrates the value of having a process in the right place at the right time. It also demonstrates the speed at which a small, hungry company can operate. Nobody in the steel business could have accomplished this task in six months, and in six months the customers would have done it themselves as did our customers a few years later by copying the Allvac furnace.

In 1961 Allvac added many other profitable products. The new products combined with an efficient shop, trained workers, and a lean and hungry attitude caused a steep rise in profits. The energetic young men took their jobs seriously and were the main reason that Allvac lived and thrived in the big league of super alloys and exotic metals.

And in 1961 all things came together. We earned $242,000 or 47c per share, as illustrated on the cover of the annual report—fig. I.

The profit information leaked before the annual report was released, and the public and brokers again renewed their interest in Allvac. The brokers extrapolated the 47c per share, and in a typical fashion predicted $1.00 for 1962 and $1.50 for 1963. Brokerage houses do the public an injustice when they practice this kind of clairvoyance with public companies.

After our bonanza year, several brokerage houses took notice and began to tout Allvac stock. The price rose to $14 per share, thirty times earnings—eventually even Merrill, Lynch noticed. Ed Gaskins, president of the local bank, smiled and loaned Allvac $25,000 for ninety days. Ed Gaskins also, with Cy Campbell at North Carolina National Bank in Charlotte, loaned me $50,000 to exercise Allvac options. Naturally, the banks held the shares with a market value of $500,000 as collateral.

I was bubbling with confidence, perhaps overconfidence, and launched a massive future planning conference. Everybody got involved. My objective was simple—to earn $1 a share. To do this I knew we had to change from a "one boss" company to an organization with a secondary layer of management. I knew we would suffer temporarily but for the longer pull we would "fund" new management for future growth to obtain $1 a share.

Oliver had always needled me about my "Kingship" attitude and had suggested an executive V.P., so I hired my friend of long standing from G.E. of Schenectady, Dick Fairly. Dick was a fast rising young man at G.E. He was one of very few selected to go to Harvard for a year of Advance

ALLVAC METALS COMPANY
Nineteen Hundred Sixty One Annual Report

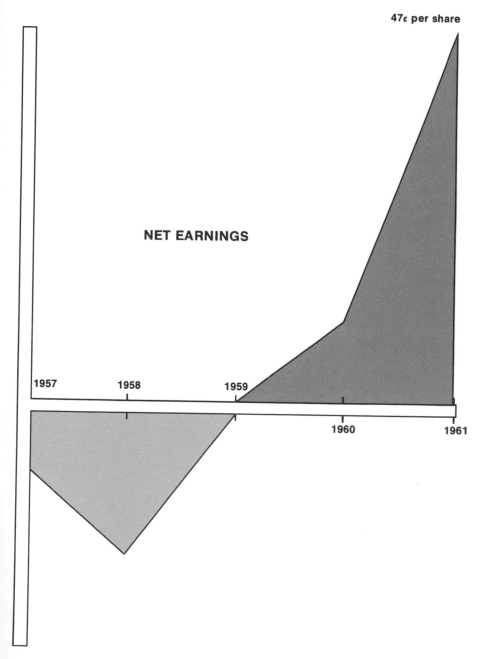

Fig. 1

Management training and he later attended the internal G.E. Management School—a bright man and a solid engineer and now a trained professional manager. Shortly after he came he invited me to a meeting he was holding with the magnet department, but I had to meet one condition. Dick said, "You must agree not to make any 'Bing—Bang' decision if you attend."

I realized then that the new organization plan was working but slowing down action.

We were quick to come to grips with problems. The magnet business we had entered soured when the Japanese decided to export magnets to the United States. At the time we entered the magnet business a particular magnet for a large loud speaker sold for $1.03. Two years after the Japanese competition appeared the price of that magnet was 53c. We decided it would be better to concentrate our efforts and money on other exotic metals. We sold our magnet company, which had always been kept separate, to Crucible Steel at a handsome profit.

The deal with Crucible was unusual: we agreed to purchase a new plant site for them in Monroe, construct a new building, transfer all the equipment and the personnel to the new plant and start up the operation for them—all in three months' time. That was accomplished, to Crucible's surprise, by an unusually capable engineer we had hired in 1958, Gary Mills.

Gary Mills dropped out of Georgia Tech after one year because he couldn't afford to return. We hired him at $1.00 an hour and encouraged him to continue his engineering at night school in Charlotte and by correspondence courses. Gary applied himself. He was smart, tenacious and vigilant. A dozen years later I was pleased and with pride I gave Gary the highest recommendations when he applied for his N. C. Professional Engineers License. Now Gary the P.E. heads up Allvac's Engineering Department with twenty assistants. One of my greatest pleasures has been to see Gary and a dozen other young men I hired at Allvac succeed and drive Cadillacs.

The other opportunities at Allvac abounded, and we had to expand. That old friend, Joe Cameron, who wrote the first check for $1,000 for Allvac shares, put me in touch with a Mr. Tenney who was the newly installed president of a small business investment company in Houston, Texas, called Business Funds.

Mr. Tenney was an interesting character, a big ruddy-faced, genial extrovert from Texas. I will always recall with a chuckle a luncheon we had with him after we consummated a deal with Business Funds. Present at the luncheon (held at the Monroe Hotel, which smells of all the meals ever cooked there and all the people who ever ate them) were Olin Nisbet, our chief broker; Ed Gaskins, our local banker, and several others from Allvac. Mr. Tenney was holding forth in lively conversation when Ed Gaskins asked:

"Mr. Tenney, what business were you in before you became associated with Business Funds?"

He replied immediately, "I was in the 'deals' business."

Ed dropped a bit of sauerkraut he was holding, and even the imperturbable Olin Nisbet put down his fork with a touch of nausea. Silence prevailed and Mr. Tenney sensed that he had said something wrong.

A "deal" in Monroe connotes a business transaction in which an eighteen year old nag is sold as a three year old colt.

Everyone relaxed when I said, "Ed, Mr. Tenney was employed as an assistant for the Murchison Brothers dealing in acquisitions."

We consummated a juicy deal with Business Funds. With our potent profit record in 1961, and with the public stock price riding well over $10 per share, we borrowed $700,000 at 7% and gave Business Funds stock options to convert the loan at $10, $12, $14, $16 and $18 per share for the next five years. Our stockholders' equity at that time was $722,000—$1.30 per share. And with the money we built the largest induction vacuum melting furnace in the world—larger than Cyclops, larger than General Electric, larger than Carpenter Steel, larger than Allegheny, larger than Latrobe, larger than Firth Sterling—larger than all. Because we learned that money alone didn't solve problems, Allvac had finally arrived on the world map of special metals companies.

We dedicated the new furnace at the annual stockholders meeting in 1962. The plan was to impress the several dozen stockholders in attendance by opening the vacuum release valve and that would make a terribly loud noise. I was a little out of character when I waxed too eloquent by saying, "I hereby dedicate this world's largest furnace to the glory of God and to the service of mankind." Then I flicked the switch for the booming noise to commence. Nothing happened! Several minutes later the trouble was found and the anticlimax went off. Our engineer at that time was a rather meek fellow for several days afterwards.

The following is quoted from a paper by my friend and colleague, F. N. Darmara, president of Special Metals. The paper was published at an International Vacuum Metallurgy Conference in 1967. It gives his very complimentary view of these times:

> *In 1945-1946, Nisbet at General Electric Company and Darmara and Huntington at NACA had small furnaces for the melting of cobalt and nickel-base alloys. About the same time, J. W. Moore at NRC had a furnace in operation for the production of pure iron and copper. By 1950-1951 the demands of the jet age and the newer higher-thrust engines strained the possibilities of conventional air-melting method to the limit. Vacuum induction melting was tried again to resolve the difficulties in meeting engine requirements. This time the seed fell on fertile ground. There has been ever since continued, ever accelerating growth and progress. By 1958 a 2.5 ton furnace was in operation and smaller furnaces were quite commonplace. It was in 1961 that J. Nisbet showed great foresight and courage by venturing into the construction of a 12,000 lb. furnace. Given the circumstances, it was a great act of faith and was greatly instrumental in minimizing the skepticism of operating personnel as to the value of vacuum induction melting as a production tool. Since then, of course, larger furnaces have been built, but this should not detract from the importance of the Nisbet venture. A 15-ton cold charge furnace is in operation and one of the following*

papers at this Symposium gives design criteria of another 15-ton furnace.

Some years back Nisbet projected a yearly vacuum induction capacity of about 1,000,000 tons for the United States by 1970. For 1967, his prediction was about 200,000 tons per annum. It is rather hard to know what USA capacity is at present. A rough estimate is about 90,000 tons per year. Considering that his estimate is based on an extrapolation from roughly 750 tons per year ten years ago, this should be considered a very good prediction. It should be realized that when this estimate was made most people considered it visionary to say the least.

Yet, when the Allvac profits in 1962 did indeed drop from 47c to 32c per share it was no longer a growth company. The brokers turned unfriendly again and found other companies to tout. The stock price dropped steadily from 30 x E or $14 in 1961 down to $3.50 (10 x E) per share in 1963, even though the company was growing by leaps and bounds in capacity, in sales, and in organizational strength, and had plans to earn $1.00 per share within three years. For the three years preceding, Allvac had been a growth company with steadily rising earnings per share, then suddenly in 1962 it was no longer a steady growth company and the public was harsh in reappraising the price per share.

Another Allvac director, Lee Loomis, a private investor on Wall Street and the representative of Business Funds on the Allvac board, regularly attended Allvac board meetings. He always spent the night before the meetings at my home. Lee, a sophisticated investor, gave me my first education in "Wall Street's" definition of growth companies. A growth company is one that has a lengthening record of consistently increasing earnings per share from quarter to quarter and year to year. If the record lasts for four or five years the price of the stock rises to an extremely high multiple of earnings, from 30 x E to even 100 x E if the growth trend is steep. If the earnings growth record is broken like Allvac's was, then the multiple and the price plummet as the Allvac price did, from $14 per share to $3.50 per share.

The second Business Funds representative on the Allvac Board was Eads Poitevant, a banker from Houston.

He was disgruntled because his options on Allvac shares were at prices ranging from $10 to $18. He pushed me hard to consider merging Allvac. That was absolutely the worst advice I ever had from an Allvac board member and I should have ignored it.

Chapter Ten

MERGER FLIRTATIONS

"Entrepreneurs see organizations as living because they often create them. They develop an affection for them but are not always surprised when the time comes for one to die, combine with a second, or change its fundamental character."
... Entrepreneurial Management ... Daily.

A number of companies in the special metals field followed the progress of Allvac after its inception in 1957, and they recognized its innovative ability and its significant position in the production of high temperature metals. When the price of Allvac stock dropped from $14 to $3.50 it became an attractive target for acquisition and the merger flirtations with other companies began.

In 1964, before Gulf & Western was as well-known as it is today, I had a call from Mr. Bluhdorn, its president. Without mincing words he asked:

"Mr. Nisbet, would you like to visit with me to discuss the possibilities of merging Allvac with Gulf & Western?"

"Allvac is not for sale," I said, "but I'd be glad to have lunch with you and discuss what you might have in mind."

In further checking on Gulf & Western I was unimpressed. It was a hodgepodge of companies ranging from automobile parts distributors to re-manufacturers of automobile bumpers for the used car market. This was before Gulf & Western acquired Paramount Pictures and changed its chrome-plated automobile bumpers image to gold-plated movie stars with big boobs.

Several weeks later I had lunch with Mr. Judelson and Mr. Bluhdorn. In the briefing before lunch I heard, for the first time, the acquirer's pitch that "Nothing changes when we acquire a company." As president of Allvac I would still run my own show while Gulf & Western would provide all the capital needed for expansion and growth.

During lunch, Mr. Judelson took a call from a Gulf & Western company. I was impressed by his part of the conversation. He was speaking with a company president about his problems. Mr. Judelson put him straight. It was obvious who had the upper hand, even though it was quite contradictory to his pitch to me on autonomy. After he hung up the look on his face showed that he realized that he had destroyed his earlier theory about autonomy in the operation of companies acquired by Gulf & Western. I couldn't resist this question:

"Was that one of your company presidents checking in?"

Needless to say, I didn't like the New York City breezes of Gulf & Western nor Mr. Bluhdorn's aggressive attitude toward buying Allvac Metals at $7 per share. I told him quite directly that Allvac Metals was a growth company and that my price was twice that per share. After lunch he said:

"Your idea of the value of Allvac is distorted. The public price is $5 and $14 is too high. We would offer you a good premium over the public price, but not $14."

I had no inclination to merge with Gulf & Western. At that time the price of Gulf & Western stock was $7.50 per share. Typical of the conglomerates in the 1960's, the price rose in a bell-shaped curve to peak at $66 in 1968 and fell back to $9.50 in 1970. In December 1972, the price was oscillating around $36 per share.

In the early 1960's Howmet (then known as Howe Sound) was an aggressive acquirer. They bought Austenal, the producers of the vitallium alloy.

Bill Weaver, then president of Howmet, heard about Allvac from mutual friends at Austenal and he called me in Monroe. He also thought our price for Allvac was too high and he never got around to structuring a specific offer, although we continued the conversations over the course of the next several months. Bill Weaver is more of a soft sell acquirer and I was somewhat disappointed that he never made a specific offer for Allvac. The price of Allvac for Howmet could have been $10, indicative of a considerably greater interest in merging with them rather than Gulf & Western.

The price of Howmet shares in 1964 was around $5. It rose to $50 in 1967 and 1968 and then fell in the typical bell shaped curve to $9 in 1970. In December 1972 the price was $13 per share.

Continental Copper & Steel owned Braeburn, an old line special steel company, and they were disenchanted with it. Thus, over a period of time they tried to either sell or merge it with another company that might manage it better.

The financial vice president of Continental Copper called on me several times and we had long discussions about the prospect of putting Allvac and Braeburn together as an operating division of Continental Copper. We didn't get very far with these discussions until I met Mr. Gordon, the president of Continental Copper. After several hours of talk Mr. Gordon folded his hands over his very large stomach and said:

"Mr. Nisbet, we would like to expand in the metallurgical business by acquiring Allvac Metals and putting it together with Braeburn as a division of Continental, and would like for you to write your own ticket as president of that division."

I said to Mr. Gordon, "That's very interesting. The price of Allvac is $14 per share."

Mr. Gordon replied, "That's too steep. I don't think Allvac is worth that much."

Two years later I had another opportunity to spend several hours with Mr. Gordon negotiating the purchase of Braeburn. At that time he offered it for sale at book value. After several hours of negotiating I offered him 25c on the dollar and he said:

"That isn't enough, Mr. Nisbet. I want book and I'll sell it to you today for book."

I told him, "My response is the same as your response to me when I asked $14 a share for Allvac a few years ago. You probably don't remember but your comment was 'That's too steep, Mr. Nisbet', so all I can say to you now is 'That's too steep, Mr. Gordon, for Braeburn Steel'."

Again the stock price of Continental Copper and Steel since that time has showed the typical conglomerate curve—from $5 in 1964 to a high of $33 in 1967. Since 1967 the price has continued down to a low of $4¾ in December 1972.

The vacuum processes which Allvac used became the standard for producing high temperature alloys between 1960 and 1965. Since most of the special steel companies had been slow in recognizing this trend they were caught with obsolete methods and had to buy ingots, the basic alloys, from Allvac. So for three years Allvac was a major supplier to several of these companies. Naturally, each of them explored with us the possibility of merging with Allvac.

The first merger exploration with this group was with Firth Sterling. In 1961 we had supplied tons of material to them and we became well acquainted with Dr. Hopkins, a vice president, and Ken Mann, the president. As competitors we also learned much about the inside operations of Firth Sterling. We had several discussions with Ken Mann about merging but found we didn't like the idea. Nothing ever came of the discussions except that Firth Sterling finally copied our facilities at their McKeesport plant, and Allvac lost a major customer. A few years later Firth Sterling was acquired by Teledyne.

Carpenter Steel sought to merge with Allvac—again to no avail. They thought our price too high. Like Firth Sterling, Carpenter installed their own facilities and we lost them as a major customer.

Next a deal was made to supply Allegheny Ludlum. Allegheny is one of the largest special steel producers; in fact they are sometimes classified as "big steel." We were a little smarter now and asked Allegheny Ludlum not to copy our facilities for at least a year and they agreed. Allegheny continued to buy for a year and at the end of that time they bought a direct competitor of Allvac, the Special Metals Company.

By 1964 vacuum processing was spilling over into the big steel industry. One of the best big steel companies, Armco, became an Allvac customer and cast an acquisition eye in our direction, but nothing concrete ever developed in these negotiations.

Vacuum melting had in a short time gone the way of all steel-making processes and we were soon confronted with an over-abundance of capacity. In 1964 Latrobe Steel and Cameron Iron topped Allvac's 15,000 pound capacity when they installed a 30,000 pound unit. Jones & Laughlin, Bethlehem, and then U. S. Steel installed vacuum treating methods for molten steel, a sure sign that vacuum processing had rapidly matured. In the future, capacity would always exceed demand and prices would fall—so typical of the steel industry.

Chapter Eleven

MERGING WITH VASCO

In October 1964 when George Roberts, President of Vanadium Alloys Steel Company (Vasco) called, I was more willing to listen and decided that my price for Allvac might now be more reasonable. This attitude is neatly expressed by Ellis in his book, *Institutional Investing*. He said, "The unknown future is what frightens mergers into being."

Roberts asked, "Jim, would you be interested in considering merging Allvac with Vasco?" Typically, his conversation didn't even slow down after that question, but he talked on for several minutes selling the idea of serious exploratory merger discussions.

I said to him, "Before we go on with this conversation you must recognize that Allvac is a growth company and therefore the price for Allvac must be a high multiple of earnings, say 20 x E, significantly higher than a steel company multiple, say 10 x E. I might add further that the book values of the two companies have nothing to do with merger values."

Roberts said he completely understood my viewpoint and would still like to get together for discussion. As the first step he suggested that he'd like to send down his troop of officers to inspect us. At first I questioned this approach but I didn't say anything because it seemed to be a great opportunity for us to sell his officers, whom I knew. None of them had ever seen our plant. Each probably had the idea that we operated a 10,000 foot pilot plant, whereas at this point we had developed quite a metal manufacturing campus with 200,000 square feet of buildings, offices, and labs.

The Vasco officers visited us the following week. It was obvious from their questions when they were picked up at the airport that they would be surprised when they saw the Allvac facility. We knew beyond any question that the Roberts troops would give George a glowing report.

George Roberts is a handsome, ambitious, and very capable business executive with unusual charm and charisma. I had known him for about twenty-five years, first as a fellow metallurgist. He was always a prominent technical man, having been elected president of the American Society for Metals when only thirty-five years old.

At this time Allvac had completely invested the capital made available by the loan of $700,000 from Business Funds the year before, and needed more working capital to keep up with its opportunities. Vasco had no debt and Allvac had loads of it. The day after George arrived in Monroe for our preliminary negotiations, I said to him:

"George, I believe if you give Allvac your available capital resources and practically all of your cash flow to invest in our unlimited opportunities, we should be able to grow and expand in new metals businesses outside steels and beyond special high temperature alloys. If we can agree on a price we might make a deal. We should have twenty times the average of the last two years' earnings plus next year's projected earnings. The public value of Vasco is approximately what the public consistently says the steel industry is worth: namely ten times the average of the last five years' earnings record or about its book value."

On George's first visit to Allvac in Monroe we got along well in our four or five hour discussion. We had a good preliminary understanding that might soon result in a deal. He, too, was surprised at the scope of our campus.

During his visit I made the following points:

1. The name of the merged company has to be changed to reflect an ambitious new enterprise. Vasco metals was suggested.
2. There must be suitable management contracts and the position of Allvac's management in the merged company must be substantial.
3. Allvac must continue to operate autonomously.
4. The objectives of the combined companies must be greater than the two alone.
5. We must aggressively pursue opportunities to acquire other companies.

During the next visit with Vasco at Latrobe we agreed on a deal at about $6 per Allvac share, 20 x E, in Vasco stock at its public price, about 10 x E.

The exchange involved 0.173 shares of Vasco stock for each share of Allvac stock, or 97,033 Vasco shares. Since Vasco was paying a dividend, the Allvac stockholders received 26c on the equivalent Allvac shares in dividends.

In retrospect, this merger was a very constructive deal for Vasco. They acquired a company engaged in a special, rapidly-growing high temperature alloy business, even though the result was a slightly negative effect on Vasco's earnings per share. This is in contrast to conglomerate acquisitions (further developed later) because the conglomerate never makes an acquisition which results in a negative effect on earnings.

The day after the directors of both companies approved the Vasco-Allvac plan to merge, we brought in bulldozers and commenced with another major expansion program, purely on the basis of a verbal agreement with Roberts that Vasco would immediately assign Allvac one million dollars for expansion.

A few weeks later at the first get-acquainted meeting in Monroe between the officers of Vasco and Allvac, the late Henry Hudson, then Vasco sales vice president, observed all the activity—ground being moved, footings being poured, and a new lake being built on the Allvac company campus—and he commented:

"My goodness, George, the Vasco stockholders have not finally approved the merger and the boys here have got the first year's plan half done. We approved a major project at Vasco eight or ten months ago and we haven't even placed orders for the equipment yet. Never in my life have I seen such a contrast in decisive action. These guys have the spirit of entrepreneurs."

So we merged with Vasco in 1965 and the Allvac management undertook the difficult task of molding our spirited company with a "ho hum" steel company.

An interesting question was raised in an early Vasco board meeting when I learned that Vasco owned a portfolio of over one million dollars of other companies' common stock. Wasn't buying stock in other companies a discouraging admission that other companies were better than Vasco? Why not buy Vasco stock with that cash or preferably seek opportunities for expansion? Buying stock in other companies has a liquidation connotation. It breeds stagnation when it is pointed to with pride by a board of directors. The attitude of the board was to be "safe" in stock of other companies rather than risk innovative investments within the company. All viable companies cry out for more capital to pursue what should be an ever-present stockpile of opportunities limited only by cash. This was, of course, the basic reason that we joined Vasco—"We take your cash and pursue our opportunities." Although this was the agreement with Roberts, the Vasco board apparently hadn't yet received the message and were loathe to cash in their portfolio.

The first project I undertook with Vasco was to continue the negotiations that they had started some months before to acquire General Electric—I like to exaggerate that way. We did not attempt to acquire the entire General Electric company but only the small section then located in Detroit, the same vacuum melting pilot plant which I had started while at General Electric ten years before. General Electric had continued to operate this pilot plant on a laboratory basis. The equipment was essentially the same that I had purchased while at the General Electric research lab.

In two sessions with the manager of this General Electric section and with one or two layers of the hierarchy above him, I was able to make a deal for the equipment and inventory and contracts. In addition to vacuum melting, this section had a small pilot plant in powder metallurgy. We were able to sell that for approximately what we had paid for the entire section. The small vacuum melting plant was moved to Allvac at Monroe and has been operated as a laboratory and pilot plant there ever since.

We also quickly consummated a deal to acquire a small testing lab in Cambridge—the same that Nick Grant, an early Allvac director, had organized.

However, soon after merging Allvac, threads of doubt began to enter my mind—perhaps Allvac with Vasco would never be as viable and as interesting as Allvac alone had been. The Vasco board seemed to be too satisfied with the status quo. I believe my own vibrations and demands for positive new directions encouraged George to act more aggressively.

I could not sit still when Vasco's huge borrowing power could be applied to reseach and development, new products, and acquisitions to turn the static climate into an atmosphere charged with growth and vitality. It was in this climate that Roberts and I took a tour on the West Coast—Los Angeles, San Francisco, and Albany, Oregon—searching for companies to acquire.

Chapter Twelve

MERGING WITH TELEDYNE

After lunch one day while visiting with the president of a San Francisco company, George took me aside and said:

"Jim, a driver is picking me up in a few minutes so I'll have to excuse myself. Try to get to the airport a little before four because I'll be with someone I want you to meet. Go ahead and continue your conversation here and see if there is any mutual interest."

Of course, whatever interest that company might have had died before George passed the first stop light on his way back to San Francisco, but I was to learn later that George had something bigger on his mind. An hour before our flight to Los Angeles, I found him at the ticket counter with a stranger.

"Jim, I'd like you to meet Henry Singleton," he said. I had never heard of Henry Singleton but I liked him immediately. We chatted for an hour before taking off for Los Angeles. George and I had a date for dinner in Los Angeles with another stubborn company president. Again we were totally unsuccessful, because George didn't seem to have his mind on that acquisition. Perhaps that was just as well since that particular company later declared bankruptcy.

The following day we visited with Steve Shelton and Steve Yih in Albany, Oregon, and discussed with them the possible merger interest between Oregon Metallurgical, which specialized in titanium, and with Wah Chang, which specialized in the zirconium business. Both had growing businesses in these two metals. (The complex Wah Chang story continues in Part IV.)

On the plane from Portland to Pittsburgh George told me that Henry Singleton was president of Teledyne, Inc., and was anxious to merge Vasco with Teledyne. Apparently, Henry had outlined several intriguing possibilities the day before at San Francisco. At first I was lukewarm because I thought of Teledyne as a soldering iron electronic company, but as I learned more I liked the prospects of a "go go"

Teledyne, and I became very enthusiastic about the possibilities of a merger.

George and Henry Singleton had been roommates at Annapolis and during their freshman year they had a math course together. George once told me that Henry was the number one student in the class while George himself had finished second. This was the first time in my long association with Roberts that he ever admitted to me, or probably to anyone else, that he was number two. I suppose it was an early indication of the respect he held for Singleton.

They kept in touch with each other during the ensuing years. Henry, after obtaining his Doctorate from M.I.T., worked for about six months at the General Electric research laboratory in Schenectady. I was also there at that time but never recall having met him. He was in physics and I was in metallurgy. He later told me that that period of his career was the most boring he had known. The habit of tea at three-thirty was too stultifying for a man of his energy and imagination. I remembered the atmosphere of the laboratory with similar feelings.

Henry never had or pretended to have the public image of Roberts. Henry is a brilliant analytical business man and George is a charming extrovert.

Following our California visit, Singleton pursued Roberts on a daily basis by telephone. During this time George and I agreed that Vasco's future would be greatly improved by merging with Teledyne, with Singleton as the chief executive officer, entrepreneur, and "conglomerateur" of the combined companies. So Roberts and I developed strategies to sell the idea to the Vasco board.

Vasco's book value was close to its public price, 10 x E. Teledyne sold at forty times earnings. Teledyne was listed over the counter—Vasco was listed on the New York Stock Exchange. Teledyne was a fresh upstart—Vasco was a stable, fifty-year old, dividend-paying enterprise. Teledyne was heavily in debt, Vasco had $1 million cash in the bank and several million dollars in stocks.

Singleton's plan to make George Roberts president of Teledyne was revealed early in the merger discussions. It was also agreed that I would be vice president of the material group of companies. That suited me fine because I would continue to be a major stockholder in the combine and manage the metals businesses, including Vasco, Allvac, and many others to be acquired.

But I wondered, how does an ancient steel company like Vasco, that has basked in corporate success and grown stale, become subordinate and adjust to a four year old newcomer like Teledyne?

Several of the older members of the Vasco board were only lukewarm or even skeptical about merging with Teledyne. Lynn Smith, one of the few aggressive directors, and I helped to get the best deal from Teledyne. At a Holiday Inn outside Pittsburgh, with George Roberts arbitrating and Henry Singleton waiting in a nearby motel five miles away, we spent an interesting evening. Frequent communiques were exchanged between motels and at least two visits by Henry took place before the deal jelled, then he came to our motel at a late hour for dinner.

Vasco had paid a common stock dividend for years. It was essential that the deal be structured so that the dividend would not only continue but be increased to at least partially compensate for the wide differences in the price earnings ratios of the two companies. It was also essential that the price offered in the Teledyne share exchange be greater than the public price of Vasco shares. Both major features of the exchange of stock were accomplished when Teledyne issued a new $3\frac{1}{2}\%$ convertible preferred. The following, quoted from Roberts' letter to Vasco stockholders May 6, 1966, shows the pre-merger and post-merger results.

"Prior to the first announcement of the merger, Vasco common stock had been trading on the New York Stock Exchange at a price between $18 and $22 per share. On March 7, 1966, announcement of the agreement in principle to merge with Teledyne was made. From April 15 to May 2, 1966, our stock has been trading in the range of $38⅝ to $41¾ per share. The dividend rate of $3.50 on the Teledyne preferred will be equivalent to $1.167 for each Vasco share now held, a 30% increase over the $0.90 dividend currently being paid on Vasco shares."

The public naturally gave overwhelming approval for the acquisition of Vasco by Teledyne. They said that Vasco shares were worth twice as much when converted into Teledyne paper. The equivalent value of the old Allvac shares in Teledyne paper would be about $12 and the dividend 34c, a 34% return on an original investment of $1 in Allvac stock. This rosy picture was to continue for several years before the great expectations of the public soured with the future decline in the performance of Teledyne.

Looking at this merger another way, the disparity in values of Teledyne and Vasco is emphasized. Vasco earned $3,415,000 in 1965 whereas Teledyne earned $5,104,000. Vasco was to contribute 40% of the combined earnings but received only 20% of Teledyne stock. Teledyne had $30 million in debt and $46 million in book value (a ratio of 1 to 1.5) whereas Vasco had only $5 million in debt and about $30 million in book value (a ratio of 1 to 6.6). Obviously, Vasco made a huge plus contribution in the combination balance sheet and earnings, and a huge sacrifice in the number of shares received.

I suggested to Henry Singleton that Vasco, a 10 x E steel company, would be burdensome to Teledyne, a 40 x E growth company. Vasco would represent a significant 30% of Teledyne's total sales following the merger and I thought the high multiple on Teledyne stock would alter when Teledyne acquired the low growth Vasco. Henry thought not. The drag of Vasco did not show until two years later because Teledyne continued to acquire earnings to compensate for "no growth" Vasco—and of course Allvac continued to grow, though its relative contribution was small.

The last Vasco board meeting before the stockholders had approved the Teledyne-Vasco merger was held at Allvac in Monroe. I thought the occasion auspicious enough to invite all of the board members and their wives to dinner at my home outside Charlotte. Also, I set up a meeting of seventy or eighty prominent businessmen for lunch the following day at the North Carolina National Bank penthouse restaurant, with Henry Singleton as guest speaker. I sent Henry and his wife a special invitation to the board member dinner and luncheon meeting. He never answered my letter. Two days prior to the meeting, when George and I were getting everything prepared, we made a special appeal that he come. His comment was that he was very busy, but would try to come for the dinner since all of the arrangements had been made.

The Vasco plane was scheduled to pick up Henry at the Atlanta airport and fly him directly to the strip in my back yard at Aero Plantation in time for dinner at eight o'clock. At 8:30 the Vasco pilot called from Atlanta and said he was unable to find Singleton. Much later the pilot called and said he had located him and they would be landing in fifty minutes. An hour later they landed, without Mrs. Singleton. Needless to say, the other ladies were disappointed.

The next morning Henry visited Allvac for the first and last time and was pleasantly surprised and impressed. Then we went to Charlotte for the luncheon. George Roberts, in his very effective way, introduced Henry. Henry gave a twenty minute report on Teledyne and the group was disappointed that he had to jet back to California and didn't have time for questions.

A few weeks later, during the two or three day meeting, while the lawyers and C.P.A.s were consummating the Teledyne-Vasco merger, I had an opportunity to talk with Singleton at the Duquesne Club in Pittsburgh. I asked him about the beginning of Teledyne. He talked freely about his experience at Litton and how he and George Kozmetsky put up $225,000 each to organize a new company that would grow to be one of the great manufacturing and financial corporations. At that time the annual sales of Teledyne were $86 million. Vasco added $50 million. I was very impressed by the confidence Henry Singleton expressed in Teledyne becoming a $1 billion international company. Teledyne sales peaked in 1970 at $1.3 billion.

Prior to buying Vasco, most of their acquisitions had been small growth companies. Vasco was not a fast grower, except for its Allvac division, but it did have the cash, a good balance sheet, and credit that Singleton could not resist. Vasco also had George Roberts, badly needed by Singleton to front his growing empire. That alone was probably valuable enough to risk the other adversities of merging "Transistors" with "Steel." I was also intrigued with the alternative challenges a merger presented to me: to continue to try to move the immovable steel businesses or to transfer its cash to growth metals other than steel.

The merger was a definite upward step in those terms and the beginning of a shift by Teledyne from growth to stability, but also a step down in terms of potential future growth in earnings per share for Teledyne. Aided by more acquisitions of stale companies, the merger later drove nails in the coffin of Teledyne's earnings per share growth. However, the merger enabled Teledyne to borrow more than it could possibly borrow before, so two definite short-term pluses resulted: (1) the cash was immediately drained out of Vasco and used in companies like Allvac that had opportunities for expansion, and (2) much more money, perhaps $50,000,000, could be borrowed to buy new growth companies. It looked like a fine formula when Teledyne could pay 10 x annual earnings for Vasco stock with Teledyne stock selling at 40 x annual earnings, but the coin had another side, well explained by Charles D. Ellis in *Institutional Investing*:

> *"Probably the worst kind of merger in terms of its impact on long-term investment value occurs when a company whose shares are valued in terms of its assets (Vasco) merges with a company whose shares are valued in terms of its growth in earnings (Teledyne). At first these arrangements always look good and attractive; the growth company will have more assets to employ creatively and the asset company will have more dynamic management, and so investors expect to see faster real growth in earnings and a multiplied gain in share value as the price earnings ratio rises. It doesn't work that way for long. In fact, the usual result is the reverse of what was expected. Managements capable of developing highly profitable uses of capital have never been much restricted by lack of money, so the influx of redundant capital doesn't make much difference in their ability to generate good business opportunities and growth in earnings. The Management's skill, imagination and drive are the real sources of earnings growth, so with more shares sharing each increment of a management-created growth the per share earnings growth usually slows noticeably.*

Meanwhile, the per share asset values have been divided among so many more shares that this is usually no longer an adequate support to the share prices. As a result, the probabilities are that the asset-and-growth merger will cross-sterilize rather than cross-fertilize the constituent companies and that the long-term investments results will be adverse."

The merger of growth companies like Allvac and Wah Chang with asset companies like Vasco and Firth Sterling eventually caused cross-sterilization, which is reflected today in Teledyne's flat earnings per share. The growing companies Teledyne acquired tended to be small, and the slow-growing or even non-growing companies tended to be large. The large units in the conglomerates eventually prevailed.

Teledyne was one of several dozen acquisitive, multi-industry companies that came to be tagged as conglomerates during the 1960's. It grew from just a vision in Singleton's mind in 1960 to a billion dollar company in 1970 by following an aggressive acquisition format and gobbling up other companies. In 1966 when we were negotiating to merge with Teledyne I extrapolated the growth of Teledyne sales during its steepest climb. I found that Teledyne sales would exceed the Gross National Product in about fifteen years if it continued that heady growth rate. I showed this to Singleton and suggested to him that his problem had shifted away from acquiring to controlling the widely diverse group of maverick companies already acquired. He preferred to keep his own counsel on this subject and didn't like to talk about it.

Part III
CONGLOMERATE V.P. -
HIERARCHY OF TELEDYNE

Chapter Thirteen

NOTHING BUT EVERYTHING CHANGES

"The overbreeding and interbreeding of executives is the root of the fashion that reached its apotheosis at the end of the 1960's—the corporation decentralized on product lines, the management responsibility devolved to profit centers, bound together by tight financial controls and meticulous forward planning...With the rose colored spectacles off, the system can be seen as a monumental bureaucracy, with veins made of paper, subject to blood clots at any point.". . .Robert Heller

Following the Teledyne and Vasco deal, George Roberts called.

"Congratulations, Jim. At the board meeting today you were elected Vice President of Teledyne."

Since he, too, was in line for congratulations as President of Teledyne, I responded accordingly. He replied:

"You're premature. I wasn't elected today. The board is meeting again tomorrow."

I was surprised. It was clearly understood by the Vasco board that George Roberts would become president. In fact, it was an important part of the merger deal. It not only indicated Singleton's desire to have George as President; it also assured me that the chief operating officer of Teledyne would continue to be the spokesman for capital in the metals versus electronics business. At this time, Singleton was President and Chairman, and George Kozmetsky, who with Singleton founded Teledyne, was Executive Vice President. Kozmetsky was oriented toward the academic community and I believe he was uncomfortable in the rough and tumble world of operating the business.

I reminded Roberts of Vasco's position and encouraged him to push the issue the following day. The next night he called and said that the situation had worked out satisfactorily and that he was named President. Kozmetsky left shortly afterward and is now head of the business school at the University of Texas. He remains on the Teledyne board and, not incidentally, continues to be one of the largest stockholders in Teledyne, second only to Singleton.

The press release that first announced Teledyne's acquisition of Vasco stated: "Teledyne and Vasco merge. Present management will be retained." Merging implies equality between two companies, but the fact was that Vasco had sold out to Teledyne.

A merger consultant once said that when a company acquisition man comes around and makes the pitch that "Nothing will change," the proper question to ask is, "How many seconds will that last after the sellout and the final consummation papers are signed?"

In a few weeks everything at Vasco changed.

George Roberts left and became president of Teledyne in Los Angeles. I became a vice president of Teledyne and absentee "corporate president" of Vasco. Henry Wimmersburger was brought in and titled "operating president." Perhaps two presidents are better than one. The Vasco board of directors—all twelve of them—disappeared. An interesting question arose from this predicament: What had the board done before? One day they were needed and the next day they were not. The substitute was me—the Teledyne group executive. Smart young men at Vasco started to seek employment elsewhere when they sensed that Vasco could not compete for capital with other more dynamic companies. They had already experienced the problem with the Allvac merger. All cash was transferred to the Teledyne account and certificates in a substantial stock portfolio were plucked from Vasco lock boxes. And United Steel Workers got busy. "O. K., fellows," the union organizers said, in effect, "The president of Vasco, a local citizen and churchman, has sold out to foreigners in California who will bleed your company and might fire you. Let us protect your interests." Roberts flew in to make a few speeches to the workers but he was now an absentee president at Teledyne residing on the Avenue of the Stars in California. After a sixty year business life without a union, Teledyne now lost to the United Steel Workers. The historical profits that Vasco had enjoyed for many years began to deteriorate on that day. USW, in asserting itself, sapped the time and profitable efforts of foremen, superintendents, managers, and officers, and the Vasco management was discouraged and unaccustomed to competing for capital on a rigid return formula.

On the day following my election as vice president of the materials companies, I appeared in my office at Allvac as usual at 8 a.m. Ted Franks, taking over as president there, had an office next door. Ted had been with Allvac a couple of years as vice president of technology.

A man of few words, he came in and said:

"Congratulations! You know, Jim, the situation has changed. You and I know that every man in the Allvac organization was hired by you. I cannot run this place in your presence and I'd suggest you move your office out of Allvac."

I moved my office to Charlotte the next week.

My next visit was to Vasco. Vasco's newly installed operations president, Henry Wimmersburger, said:

"You're the boss now, Jim, and I know you have many new programs, innovations, and proposed changes in the organization."

I replied, "Henry, I have only one specific recommendation today. Drop your membership in the American Iron and Steel Institute. That would save Vasco several thousand dollars a year and about two hundred man-days per year that are spent attending various American Iron and Steel Institute committee meetings. Even more importantly, we would get rid of the stale steel influence which comes through this club. Paraphrasing Henry Ford: 'The American Iron and Steel Institute is too familiar with the impossible.' "

Remember that George Roberts had just departed for the Avenue of the Stars in California to be president of Teledyne. Yet his spirit was still at Vasco and I supposed shreds of that spirit would continue for years. I was not surprised by Wimmersburger's immediate comment:

"You and I have talked about this some before. I don't

completely disagree with you, but what would George Roberts think?"

"Henry, let's try to get off on the right foot," I said. "I respect George, as you do, but we have to realize that he is gone and that it is up to us to chart the course of this company. I doubt that he will disagree. While our men are talking to each other in American Iron and Steel Institute committee meetings, the Japanese and the Swedes are out in our field selling tool steel. As Willkie said, 'It's one world', and I believe it will continue to be more and more one world in the steel business, the Institute notwithstanding. While the Institute people are having audiences with Congressmen, the Congressmen are busy voting more money to build steel mills in Pakistan and probably in Bangladesh. Scrap dealers in the United States are building mini-steel mills miles away from the steel centers and producing bars and angles at five man-hours per ton, while big steel requires eleven. The operators of these mini-mills are entrepreneurs and very aggressive and competitive. As Ken Iverson, president of Nucor, a small mill in South Carolina, told me, "We don't have time for the American Iron and Steel Institute."

Needless to say, Vasco is still a member of A.I.S.I., but last year I doubt if the company even earned enough to pay the dues.

The greatest control imposed by Teledyne on Vasco and other acquired companies was in financial planning and reporting. This general control is discussed in the book *Financial Performance of Conglomerates*, by Harry H. Lynch:

> *"But the small and sometimes not so small acquisition appears very often not to have developed this kind of planning and control. Each new acquired subsidiary is required to adapt to this system as soon as possible, and for some it is a major transition. Many simply are unable to do it with their existing personnel, and temporary assistance from the corporate group is combined with the hiring of a controller and perhaps other financial personnel. In such situations it is rare that the subsidiary manager is initially pleased. Preparing an annual financial plan for the first time is not only time-*

consuming and frustrating; without any experience in the process it is probably not meaningful when completed. However, once the transition is finally made and the new system in operation, typically after three or four quarterly cycles, many of the subsidiary managers appear to consider it very valuable."

Vasco operated for years, as many small and medium sized companies do, with unsophisticated financial controls. Teledyne wanted tight operation. At my first Vasco board meeting two years earlier, I had been surprised that each inside director in charge of a division of the company followed a simple reporting system of sales only; no profits, no budget plan, no long range planning, and little capital planning. The most important single thing the good conglomerate does is to demand that each of its companies make a detailed budget with profit and capital planning forecast. Each month the results are carefully compared to the plan. I was very conscious of this demand because at Allvac we had developed financial planning and reporting which compared favorably with Teledyne's systems. When Allvac joined Vasco, I tried to impose the Allvac system but I got nowhere, because, you see, Vasco had bought Allvac.

The Teledyne system caused turmoil at Vasco, compounded when the Vasco treasurer left to join George Roberts' staff in Los Angeles. We brought in a fresh financial man and tried harder.

I believe in reasonable but far-reaching goals in planning, and I asked the Vasco officers to extend themselves in process and product innovations. The first plans were disappointing. They were at the same stale pace: sales equal to last year's, no new products, no new processes, and no innovations. But typical of the steel industry, the manufacturing vice president had included massive plans to spend more capital—plans related only to what competitive companies were spending. He wanted $5 million to "keep up with the Joneses;" yet according to the sales plan no capacity increase was needed.

I said to him, "The trouble is that steel companies are capital hogs, all copying one another!" And I dreamed up the following satire to make the point.

87

Chapter Fourteen

A SATIRE ON THE STEEL INDUSTRY

This is a hypothetical board of directors meeting of a typical big steel company. Let's call it "UNITED STEEL CAPACITY UNLIMITED CORPORATION."

The meeting was called to order.

I. The first item on the agenda was smog pollution from the downtown Pittsburgh blast furnaces. Following a thorough report from a committee of eighteen medical experts, it was discussed for more than two hours. The board decided that the committee should continue to meet for another year and study the problem in greater depth, and during the ensuing year issue quarterly press releases on clean air in the Golden Triangle.

II. The second item was a 30% raise for the United Steel Workers and a price increase of 10% on all products. — Approved.

III. Next were officer bonuses for the year totaling $3.7 million and the simultaneous announcement of a cut in the quarterly dividend from 8c to 5c per share. — Approved.

IV. Then came the capital requests from the engineering department for a new blast furnace to cost $50 million. Several pertinent questions were raised and discussed by the members:

The lady member of the board asked about the possibility of more pollution from the new blast furnace. She also asked if space to install the new equipment was available in the Allegheny River Plant. The chief engineer was called in, and he had a ready answer.

"Recent statistics show that the gas effluent from new blast furnaces has been reduced by 2/10 of 1% from the old style equipment, that the number of houses in Pittsburgh that are air conditioned is increasing, and further, that the solution to this problem is air conditioners that produce cleaner air at the source of breathing. There is not enough land to install the equipment, but plans call for filling in ten acres further out into the Allegheny River."

Then an 80 year old Director spoke in favor of the investment because he had overheard the president of Bessie Steel say that they planned to install a new blast furnace that year. United Steel Capacity Unlimited Corporation could not fall behind in capacity.

The Director from Merrill, Bull & Real Estate spoke up and inquired about present blast furnace utilization and about the new iron making innovations that Allegheny River Steel was experimenting with. He had read something about this in a recent analyst's report on the steel industry. The engineering vice president spoke:

"Gentlemen, we are now operating our five blast furnaces at only 60% of capacity, but that is really not pertinent. It takes five years to build, install, and debug a new blast furnace. Therefore, if we do not start a sixth furnace now we might be in very serious capacity shortage when business improves and if, in the meantime, imports are cut off by our Institute representatives in Washington.

"Furthermore, the new processes being tried by small steel companies are not interesting and are too expensive. The blast furnace will be around a hundred years.

"For example, Sir Henry Bessemer demonstrated the feasibility of continuously casting steel in 1850, and even today that process represents only 1% of steel production by small-fry steel companies. The steel industry should be slow in taking on new innovations."

Then a 75 year old retired Director who lunched each day at the Duquesne Club reinforced the engineer's report because it coincided with similar plans he had overheard from other competitors, including Wheeling & Dealing Steel Corp., when he eavesdropped on their luncheon meeting a few days before.

The chairman put the question to a vote, and it unanimously passed.

Before the meeting was adjourned the chief engineer said:

"By the way, gentlemen, I forgot to put this in the formal capital request, but we must come back later this year and vote another $50 million for the auxiliary equipment and filling in the river. I just wanted you to be aware of our long range capital plans."

The board adjourned to the cocktail lounge and drank martinis before having the famous Duquesne Club crabmeat hozell as an appetizer before dinner.

The Baptist minister from Birmingham was excused before dessert of mocha ice cream so that he could take the company jet back to Birmingham in time for a labor rally. Incidentally, he was to be introduced over closed circuit television by the able head of the Steel Workers Union from his suite in the Mountainbleu Hotel at Miami Beach.

*   *   *

Vasco capital planning improved slightly but the spirit to innovate lagged on and on.

Big steel companies are capital hogs. They have difficult long-range planning problems in capital investing because a major plant usually takes five years to build and twenty-five years to return the money. So all steel company presidents tend to be stuck with the decisions made by their predecessors who have already spent their capital. Then the next president has to do the same thing for his successor.

An extreme, slightly exaggerated contrast is the small electronics company which can buy a few soldering irons, rent a loft and be in business in a few months, and pay out in a year. Sewing machine businesses in textiles can do likewise.

Yet, the ponderous nature of big steel and its preoccupation with tonnage allows or even invites innovators to slip in with new processes which are emerging from the laboratory and are still on a poundage rather than a tonnage scale. Thus, Allvac was able to enter the industry just as many mini-steel mills, engineered for the lowest man-hours per ton, are springing up over the U. S. and the world.

Chapter Fifteen

SYNERGISM

During the conglomerate parade in the mid '60s much was written about synergism, the 2 plus 2 equals 5 notion. It ain't so:

In 1967, I set out to see if we could synergize by combining the sales department of several companies. Some of the metal companies had different customers but in many cases the customers overlapped. Also, throughout the states there was duplication in warehouses and sales offices. The situation was mapped and we brought together six of the larger company presidents to have a think session on the possibility of cooperative field sales—if General Electric could do it, why couldn't Teledyne? (Perhaps we should have said, "If General Electric does it, let's avoid it like the plague.")

I thought a good materials salesman should be able to sell a variety of materials. (If a tool steel salesman could sell one hundred different tool steels, he should be able to sell ten varieties of super alloys.) But the sales management informed me that a tool steel salesman could not sell gas turbine alloys, and vice versa.

The resistance to my plan continued to be formidable. I relented to the point of agreeing that if more than one division occupied an office they would be allowed separate entrances—a silly concession, as no customers ever call at the steel sales office anywhere, any time, and they never, never visit a warehouse. Business is done at the buyer's order desk and at the customer's engineering department.

The only way Teledyne material companies could be synergized in sales would have been to take on new sales managers who believed that it could be done and to spend two or three years developing the concept. That procedure, however, would have violated Teledyne's idea that the company's president is king.

The company president as king could not cooperate with other companies in selling because it would inevitably cause some loss of his control. I notice, however, that as time passes and old timers leave, there is a definite trend toward less kingship by the president of a decentralized division and more operating bossmanship by group vice presidents. In turn, each group takes on a staff of overlords and centralization sets in.

There is probably a point somewhere between the Teledyne extreme of decentralization and complete centralization that is the most practical way to operate. Older companies such as General Electric tend to shift in degrees of centralization like a pendulum—swinging too far in centralizing by one president and then too far in decentralizing by another. The proliferation of staff positions is a byproduct of this in all large and older companies. A new company like Teledyne, however, is not yet mature enough to have developed an office filled with a corporate staff. Teledyne is housed in only one floor of an office building, yet General Electric, even after Cordiner's decentralization regime, still maintained an entire building for staff personnel at 570 Lexington Avenue, as well as a few buildings in Schenectady and at other plants for the same purpose.

Later on I enjoyed making this point when reluctant entrepreneurs raised questions about autonomy. The point was that experts on Teledyne's staff didn't exist. Therefore, even though there might be a desire on the part of the president or chairman or group officer to send out the troops from corporate, there were no troops to send.

Over the years Vasco's variety of high speed tool steels proliferated to several hundred and standardization was badly needed. It was like offering fifty shades of gray. We found that ten varieties could be substituted for the hundred Vasco normally marketed. And even within the ten it was quite difficult to discern large or significant difference in physical properties.

I spent a great deal of time promoting standardization as a high priority project for the technical organization. They pointed out that although such a move was theoretically possible, the sales department liked to satisfy customer idiosyncrasies by guaranteeing them a tool steel with the carbon content 1/100 of a point different from what their competitors used. Therefore, I conferred with the managers of the sales department and advocated a joint effort of standardization between the technical and sales groups.

After three or four months literally nothing was accomplished, and the task force of salesmen and metallurgists that were brought together never met more than twice. Henry Wimmersburger—a wise old guy—finally told me why: "Jim, I guess your trouble is that you don't know how to sell tool steel. You have assumed that customers and salesmen are reasonable and logical and that they want this system of standardization that you have proposed. The fact is, however, that the sales gimmicks are rampant in selling tool steel and certain names get to be sacred. Selling tool steel is not based so much on technology or performance, but on a catchy name like 'desecotized' and a good line of bullshit."

1) General Electric Research
   Dr. Holloman, Dr. Suits and Nisbet

2) Universal Cyclops Steel Company Directors

3) Allvac Metals Board of Directors

4) Allvac Metals Annual Stockholders Meeting

5) Allvac Metals Exchanging Stock With Vasco

6) Steve Yih President of Wah Chang

7) Henry Singleton, Chairman of Teledyne

8) Kay Nisbet at Aero Plantation

9) Allvac Teledyne Plant

Chapter Sixteen

INTERNAL GROWTH

It bothered me that Teledyne was unable to carry forward opportunity for expansion and growth by creating new companies based on new products and developed from within. All large companies should have new products and processes coming on, then exploit the new ideas by the creation of an entirely separate company to push them forward.

Teledyne was so busy acquiring between 1965 and 1968 that Singleton had little time to consider the creation of new divisions from within until we organized a new company called Teledyne Titanium.

Titanium is only twenty-five years old in terms of use in metallic form. I had been unsuccessful in getting Allvac interested in titanium and concluded that the only way Teledyne could advance in that field would be to create a new company to concentrate in the production and selling of titanium and its alloys. We evolved a fairly elaborate plan showing capital needs, organization needs, selling strategy, etc. (and a separate sales force, of course) to present to Roberts and Singleton.

Ted Franks, president of Allvac, reluctantly agreed to leave that job and be president of this new company. Initially he would be the only employee. His charter was to rapidly put together an organization. Ted had run a company of his own which we had acquired earlier. He was a metallurgist and had the knowledge and the entrepreneurial experience to create a new enterprise.

Even so, I approached Roberts and Singleton with trepidation. Henry's success in acquisitions with immediate gains in earnings per share left him unenthusiastic about creating a new company that would probably have to operate by deficit financing for several years. I certainly disliked the idea that I could not proceed with the plan on my own, but now they signed the checks.

Nevertheless, we had a good plan and Singleton and Roberts approved it. I called back to Monroe an hour later and set the wheels in motion to purchase the land I had already optioned for the new plant. The initial approval was for about $2.5 million, proof that Teledyne had grown to a size where it could now afford to spend some capital for the creation of new businesses from within.

Since that time, Teledyne has continued to create a few new companies and I expect, with the merger parade over, that method of growth will accelerate.

Chapter Seventeen

A TALE OF
TWO PRESIDENTS

1. A Lonesome President

Another metals company Teledyne acquired was Portland Forge. Six weeks after the acquisition Lee Hall, the president, called me:

"Jim, I'm lonesome. We've been with Teledyne six weeks. We have seen financial people here, installing their controls and reporting system. We have had a few conversations with the lawyers. But I haven't even talked to Roberts or Singleton. You are my new Teledyne boss and I haven't talked with you either."

I said, "Lee, you make me feel guilty, but I've been busy flying here, there, and yon where there are profit problems. Just a few days ago I saw your monthly performance report and you turned in the second best performance of any material company in the whole damn group. My inclination is to play it smart and stay as far away from Indiana as I can because I could do nothing that could improve your profit. However, I'll be out to see you next week if you're lonesome. If you get too lonely your profits might fall."

My responsibility to Portland Forge was to substitute for the past board of directors and, of course, if the president was lonely I had to go there quickly. I was interested in exposing Lee's unusual talent to other company presidents. He knew how to earn 10% on sales in the forge shop business.

2. A Well Paid President

Picco, a precision casting company in Los Angeles, was managed by Ralph Miller, an energetic man. At that time he had the greatest profit ability of any plant manager I have known. Therefore, I tried to learn his technique and spread it to other metal companies.

Lynn Smith, an old friend who was also a director of Vasco, had sold Picco to Teledyne. Lynn continued to manage Picco on a part-time basis. How could I spread the talents of Picco to others? It was the highest profit company in all the materials group—even better than Portland Forge—and sometimes turned in 20% profit on sales.

One day George Roberts called and requested that I visit Picco.

"Jim, you ought to come out and talk to Ralph Miller at Picco. He has some things to review."

I told him I'd be glad to, but reminded him that Lynn Smith was there every day.

"He has been running the company for years and knows how to do it," I said. "I saw their profit report last week and it is better than any other company we own. Do you realize that?"

George said, "Yeah, I realize that, but there is a problem. You know when I bought Picco I had some tough negotiations. I had to pay Lynn Smith a pretty good price, but the problem was to persuade Ralph Miller to stay. We had to make a deal with him for his continuation of profit participation, a deal Lynn had given him for a number of years. We've got a real problem now because that fellow makes about as much money as I do as president of Teledyne. That doesn't seem right."

"I guess we do have a problem, but you made the deal and you're right there in Los Angeles," I told George. "Why don't you do something about it?"

George responded patiently, "No, you've always raised hell with me when I meddled around in your companies. It's your problem now. Come on out here and do something about it."

I conceded and later spent a day with Lynn and Ralph, and as you might guess, I accomplished nothing. Ralph's salary and bonus arrangement remained the same, as I thought it should. When a conglomerate gobbles up an entrepreneur with its big company ideas and Harvard business school management notions, it tends to lose the entrepreneur as an employee very quickly because of management strings and stingy ideas of pay.

Unless there is an opportunity for large monetary gain by managers in Teledyne during the next decade, the public value of Teledyne stock ten years hence will not be worth much more than it is today. With mediocre pay there will be mediocre managers. Just as the big companies have grown into big bureaucracies, so will the big conglomerates, and neither can tolerate or accommodate the itch of an entrepreneur within their organizational maze. They close off the avenues and paths for innovative managers to find riches within the company. Then, in turn, they cast aside the entrepreneur in favor of the bureaucratic professional managers who are satisfied with the security of the maze and mediocre pay.

Geneen of ITT is an exception. He is not bashful in saying he makes millionaires and that seems to reflect in the continuing growth of even the giant multi-billion dollar ITT.

This is not to say that the very few top managers in large companies are badly paid. Other giants, like General Electric, probably make fifty or so vice presidents into millionaires in ten year cycles. But the price of becoming a millionaire is high. It frequently seems to mean avoiding innovations at the highest levels of incompetence in the scramble up the pinnacle of the presidency, before retiring, exhausted, to Lost Tree.

Part IV

WAH CHANG - AN INTRIGUING ACQUISITION

"Are you the seller? The morning comes to you with an instant recall of the night's deed. Along with that shock, you become aware of a cold overcast outside your window. You have an immediate feeling of dour reality, then a rumbling in the stomach and the first hint of bile in the mouth. You begin to feel your eyes bulging in disbelief at the enormity of it. You have given it all away for a pittance, married off your business, so that in the morning it is no longer all yours, as it has been almost, it seems, forever."
... *Welcome to Our Conglomerate–You're Fired!* ...
Isadore Barmash.

Each company Teledyne acquired had its own personality and history and had to adjust to many changes. Teledyne also had to make adjustments for each new acquisition. The most interesting and complex Teledyne acquistion of all was a company called Wah Chang. The negotiations to acquire Wah Chang were very complex and extended over a longer period of time than any acquisition in my experience.

Just after Allvac and Vasco merged, and before Vasco merged with Teledyne, George Roberts and I opened negotiations to buy Wah Chang. Roberts and I had set out to expand Vasco's direction toward more exotic metals. Wah Chang produced five of the new metals we were interested in—tungsten, molybdenum, zirconium, hafnium, and columbium. All these metals possessed unique properties and the potential for attractive market growth.

In our original conversation with Steve Yih, the manager of the Albany, Oregon, plant, we learned two important facts: first, Wah Chang was in default on a $6 million note to the First National City Bank of New York and the bank had taken control from the owners, the K. C. Li family; and second, deep animosity had developed between Yih and the Wah Chang board. Yih's objective at this time was to find new financing so he could take control.

Wah Chang has many meanings in Chinese depending on the imagination of the individual. It may mean "blossoming flower," "exciting future," "beautiful garden," or "the horizons of unexpected developments," but to me it carries a connotation of oriental intrigue and management insurrection.

The following quote from an article published in Business Week, April, 1970, hints at the complexities of this acquisition.

"Vasco brought a third wave of Teledyne acquisitions—after electronics and geophysics. It has concentrated, though not exclusively, on strengthening the company's position in materials, specifically exotic metals and alloys. The acquisition of Wah Chang Corporation earlier this year was a coup.

"Wah Chang, a leading producer of tungsten, hafnium, zirconium, columbium and other exotic metals, was a closely held company whose affairs were as inscrutable as the Far Eastern roots of its owners might suggest. 'I could write a book about that one,' says Roberts.

– – – – –

"The basic idea in management, as Singleton sees it, is to keep a cooperative spirit going in an atmosphere that encourages growth and risk. He admits the jury is still out whether it will work indefinitely.

" 'After seven years at Litton,' he observed, 'key employees started leaving to go out on their own. This is our seventh year.'

"Singleton concedes he would get very worried if defections began. But so far he is not concerned, and he is not looking for advice on the subject of making employees happy or how to manage a large company. 'I'm not going to read the book,' he says. 'I just wrote it.' "

Recently I told Henry about this book and I asked him if he would like to write a foreword to it.

"I don't know about that, Jim," he said, "but I sure would like to read it."

I guess Henry has more time for reading lately.

Chapter Eighteen

THE LI'S AND YIH

Wah Chang was started in 1916 by Dr. K. C. Li, Sr. As a young man he immigrated to this country from China. He was a metal trader during his early life. At one time he was the tungsten magnate of the world, controlling the exports of tungsten ore and metal from China and Korea. He formed a tungsten and molybdenum ore processing company in Glen Cove, Long Island.

Under the strange and complex management of Li, Sr., Wah Chang prospered and grew, specializing in these refractory metals. Other refractory metals were added when Wah Chang was awarded a contract by Atomic Energy Commission to operate the Bureau of Mines Zirconium Pilot Plant in Oregon. The A.E.C. was interested in the special and unique nuclear properties of zirconium. Then the Aircraft Nuclear Propulsion (ANP) project chose columbium and Wah Chang added columbium metal to its ken and later hafnium. Today Wah Chang is probably the most prominent company in the world producing the new and very special metals; zirconium, hafnium, columbium, tungsten, and molybdenum. Li, Sr., installed his protege, Steve Yih, as president of Wah Chang. Yih, a young engineer from Shanghai, came to the United States in 1947 and studied electrical engineering at the Polytechnical Institute of Brooklyn and later chemical engineering at New York University and Columbia. In 1953 he was hired by Wah Chang to study and redesign their electric and water supply systems at the Lincoln Mine. Dr. Li's son, K. C. Li, Jr., was about Steve's age and then a close personal friend, but he never accepted his father's many attempts to bring him into the business because his primary interest was the restaurant business. However, when Li, Sr., died in 1961, Li, Jr., deposed Steve Yih as president of Wah Chang and sent him back to Albany to operate the zirconium and hafnium plant.

Three years later Wah Chang was in desperate financial straits and in default on a $6 million loan at First National City Bank. When the bank took control, Onno Oncken, a German-born engineer and lawyer from Brazil and New

York, was loaned by W. R. Grace at the request of the bank to manage the company.

These events led me to put this question to Steve Yih at the first meeting George Roberts and I had with him.

"What would be K. C. Li, Jr.'s attitude toward selling Vasco an option on his Wah Chang shares if Vasco took over the $6 million in defaulted Wah Chang notes held by First National City Bank of New York?"

"His attitude doesn't matter," Steve responded. "He is not interested in the business. He is a playboy; he runs a restaurant in Greenwich Village, calls it 'Casey's'. He is the only Chinaman who serves French food in a restaurant with an Irish name."

Some time later when Steve and I were reminiscing about Li, Sr., I said:

"The old man never had any financial problems in the many years that he was in charge, and it puzzles me that soon after his death, First National City Bank called the Wah Chang loan."

Steve puffed on his pipe for a minute and finally said:

"I have thought about this many times, Jim, and I think I have it figured out."

I waited.

"The old man was so smart he found a way to take it with him."

Thus began my fascinating experience with the Oriental company, Wah Chang, and with the many faceted Chinaman named Steve Yih.

Steve Yih was an intriguing character. Being raised in China, he was an oriental or eastern personality. He was Americanized by an engineering education in New York City and became an astute technical man in several disciplines—chemical, mechanical and metallurgical engineering. He grew in business management and financial management as head of the Wah Chang Albany plant. In fact, Steve was chief of technology, finance and sales. Although he developed under him capable assistants in each

118

function he continued to be chief of each function and carried an unbelievable amount of information, facts and figures in his head. For example, I once tried to get to the bottom of the method or procedure for valuing hafnium inventory but was never completely satisfied or sure. He knew, and I think it was valued right, but the path used to arrive at the final numbers was complex—perhaps chop suey economics, which Steve referred to at times. Nevertheless, I think he was, and is, a man of honesty and integrity and a very warm and intellectual personality.

In a subsequent meeting with a vice president of First National City Bank we found that Steve was negotiating not only with Vasco but also with several other companies and was harrassing the bank. The bank was also negotiating separately to sell out Wah Chang. But the bank had set priorities, negotiating with their first choice, a giant electrical company, and leaving the others waiting in order: a special steel company, a big steel company, a big aluminum company, and finally Vasco. The vice president made it clear that if negotiations with the other companies were unsuccessful, we might be invited for further discussions.

We could only guess who their other companies were. Later on, I learned from Yih that they were blue chips of American industry.

First the Norton Company, then General Electric Corporation, Carpenter Steel, Armco Steel, and Harvey Aluminum. All had had serious discussions with the bank and several had advanced to the verge of a deal.

Chapter Nineteen

ACQUIRING WAH CHANG

Then George and I got the idea for a Vasco coup. Why not buy the note directly from the bank at face value and get control of Wah Chang at a low price?

By this time, zirconium had been specified as the only material for containing uranium in nuclear reactors generating electric power. Several companies were taking orders for turnkey nuclear power installations that specified zirconium. Admiral Rickover had proven the value of nuclear propulsion for submarines and ships, and zirconium and hafnium were specified for these vessels. The acquisition of Wah Chang, the world's largest producer of zirconium and hafnium, was a great opportunity for Vasco.

But a problem arose: when the proposition was presented to the Vasco board, George and I could not persuade them to take the gamble. Their immobility disappointed me, but I was not too surprised. It was a stolid group without the daring for such a deal and we could not force the step. I concluded then that the entrepreneurial approach of Allvac would not survive at Vasco.

A few months later, Vasco merged with Teledyne and the new atmosphere was refreshing. The old Vasco Board was superannuated, and Henry Singleton, a first rate entrepreneur and the chief executive officer of Teledyne, fully supported George and me in our search for new companies.

I kept in close touch with Wah Chang and early in 1967 during a telephone conversation with Oncken it became clear to me that the opportunity to acquire Wah Chang might still exist. A few days later in New York he gave me the latest financial data, showing the increased sales and profits that we had visualized during the Vasco negotiations. Wah Chang's zirconium profits were skyrocketing.

After reviewing the figures, I asked Onno, "What price?"

He had done his homework, and without hesitation he said:

"We will sell Teledyne 50% of Wah Chang for $10 million—$6 million for the bank and $4 million in working capital for Wah Chang." I knew the zirconium plant alone might be worth the price. Three other Wah Chang plants, producing tungsten in Glen Cove, molybdenum in Huntsville, and tin in Texas were somewhat questionable, but if these could break even it was a good deal.

I called Roberts and Singleton from Onno's office.

They asked, "What's the deal?"

"It's simple," I said. "$10 million for 50% interest."

"Very interesting," they said. "What is the recent financial information?"

I read the figures to them. Immediately they were interested and asked me to stand by. An hour later Henry called and again we reviewed the situation. Henry asked to speak with Onno, and they agreed to meet in Los Angeles two days later.

During the ensuing week I had several telephone conversations with George and Henry about Wah Chang, and in all of our discussions and reviews the conclusion was consistently, "Let's buy it," although Henry preferred 100% ownership.

Within the next several days the agreements were signed, and Onno agreed to continue as managing director. We debated about trying to acquire the other 50% controlled by Li, Jr., but gambled on being able to get that later.

Henry strongly believed that all acquisitions should be for 100% ownership. The prospects of the metals group of Teledyne entering the fast growing zirconium business with the auxiliary pluses of columbium, tantalum, molybdenum, and tungsten were so attractive that 50% equity was an adequate beginning. Three months later Henry was able to acquire Li's interest in exchange for Teledyne shares. The total cost of Wah Chang was about $22 million. How quickly things change in a growing enterprise—Vasco could have had control for only $6 million two years earlier.

Chapter Twenty

MORALE VERY BAD IN ALBANY, OREGON

The first changes made at Wah Chang after Teledyne acquired it stirred up a hornet's nest. On Onno's advice we maintained Li as president and dropped Steve Yih as a director, limiting him to managing the Albany plant. Onno thought that he would be troublesome in the overall Wah Chang management. We didn't have a Chinaman's chance to run Wah Chang without Steve Yih. Later on, Steve Yih told me he had abstained from voting in favor of the Teledyne offer. Steve had earlier obtained an option from the bank and Li, Jr., for himself and his employees to buy the Albany plant. Naturally, Yih was displeased and angry that Li had sold it out from under him.

Singleton, Roberts and I, as new board members, with Yih as guest only, attended the first meeting of the new board of directors. The agenda included reports from the managers of four plants: Albany, Glen Cove, Huntsville, and Texas City.

It was quite apparent that Yih's humor was poor. He was agitated and disgruntled. After hearing reports from the other managers, Steve gave a tongue-in-cheek business report and then emphasized the bad morale in the Albany zirconium plant.

Afterwards, Li took the floor and made a ten minute speech that wasn't clear to anybody. He was very much out of touch with Wah Chang.

There was a period of bewildered silence. Steve slowly removed his pipe and said:

"Shit."

Pause.

He continued, "Morale bad in Albany."

We looked at the floor, looked at papers in front of us, shuffled our feet and a few minutes later the meeting was adjourned.

Back at Kennedy airport, Steve joined Roberts, Singleton and me for a drink and reiterated his point that "morale very poor in Albany," and blamed Teledyne. He also expressed his displeasure at being removed from the Wah Chang board. Before leaving on our respective planes, we sought to appease him by agreeing to meet with him at the Albany plant two weeks later.

Within a day I received a letter from Onno stating that Li had earlier offered to reorganize Wah Chang so that the Albany management group would have an equity position in their own operation. I suggested to George and Henry that we honor this commitment to soothe management discontent and to avoid a possible management insurrection. In his letter Onno warned that the question would probably be raised at the Albany meeting. Furthermore, he suggested that we not deny or confirm the commitment until we could study the morale problem further. When we met in Albany two weeks later Steve presented his resignation. Also, he invited us to meet with twenty key members of the management group at breakfast the next morning. He told us that the management group knew of his resignation.

"Morale very bad." He was certainly not letting us miss that point.

"All twenty might resign," he warned.

We met under icy conditions. We were asked why Yih was thrown off the board, a difficult question since the action had been recommended by Onno Oncken. Onno was present and sat like a statue.

We at Teledyne still had a lot to learn about the intricacies of events leading up to the "bad morale." Later on, I found out directly from Yih, piece by piece and bit by bit more and more background information. Before this time, separately from the specific offer to Yih that he and his group be granted equity in the Albany plant, Yih had also reached advanced stages of negotiations to finance the purchase of the Albany plant through an underwriting coupled with a $1,000,000 input from employees. Naturally, it was shocking when they heard Teledyne had purchased 50% interest in Wah Chang. Yih then quickly negotiated his first offer from Carpenter Steel and a second from Armco

Steel. Both companies wanted Yih to get them into the zirconium business, with his group having an equity position in a new company.

Later we visited the plant and the atmosphere remained tense. The management group requested that we meet again, but Singleton and I had to return to Los Angeles. I sensed that we had a complex problem on our hands, so I got Roberts aside:

"I believe we have a hell of a problem, and I think I had better cancel my plans and attend this meeting with you tonight."

George thought he could solve it and said, "Jim, you and Henry go on as planned. The problem can be solved with Yih and his men."

That was Friday. Sunday George telephoned me in North Carolina and asked me to return to Albany immediately and assume management of Wah Chang. Far from being solved, the problem was now not only Yih's resignation, but the imminent resignations of the other top managers as well.

I arrived in Albany on Monday. Yih was gone. I met with Roberts and we interviewed each of the managers individually for several hours. That night and all the following day we attempted to sort out their loyalties. We soon knew Yih had a Chinese Tong. There was absolute solidarity between Yih and his men. It was impossible to mitigate the very antagonistic attitude toward Teledyne.

The second night after my arrival I was worn out and ready for a drink. Roberts and I went to Tops, a restaurant in Albany. It was a holiday and no cocktails were being served.

A stranger came over to our table and introduced himself as the manager of a small machine shop that did work for Wah Chang. He knew why we were there. He was abreast of all developments. He knew that Yih had been bumped from the board. He knew Yih had resigned. He knew the management group planned to resign. For a small consideration, he could help us keep the plant going because he said, borrowing a line from "Music Man," he "knew the territory."

125

We told him that our first problem was to find a drink. Immediately he called a waitress and whispered something to her. Thirty seconds later a bottle of Scotch appeared. George and I were dumbfounded. It was embarrassing to sit there and be briefed on the intrigue of a company which we had acquired so recently and lost control of so quickly. We talked little and listened a lot.

The following day, George had urgent business in Texas and left me as the lonesome resident manager of Wah Chang, Albany. I was there ten weeks. In the course of the first ten days, all twenty of the management group resigned in pairs. Yih's secretary resigned last—a final act of solidarity. I told them that their resignations were not accepted and work at the plant must go forward. This confused them and their reaction was to continue to work and await further instructions from Yih.

Singleton and I talked of cleaning house and replacing the plant management, but this seemed impractical to me. I was convinced that the only solution would be to honor Li's and Oncken's commitment to Yih. Henry opposed this course, urging that I accept all resignations and recruit replacements as quickly as possible. Recruiting twenty competent people to run this plant was inconceivable.

He did not insist, and I gradually started making some headway in negotiations. We persuaded Yih to join Teledyne as a consultant. He and I shared an office and became very friendly. We spent many hours talking about Wah Chang and the zirconium business, and I slowly began to understand the causes of "bad morale in Albany."

Chapter Twenty-One

THE PLOT THICKENS

The Bureau of Mines had had a station for many years in Albany. It became prominent after World War II when the technology for purifying and alloying titanium and zirconium metals was developed there.

Zirconium technology was further developed at Wah Chang, but the development of titanium took a different course when Shelton, a scientist at the Bureau of Mines, organized a new titanium company (Oregon Metallurgical) and sold shares for $1 each. Oregon Metallurgical did well during the next ten years, and the stock advanced. It was now $20 per share.

The titanium people were getting rich with equity ownership in Oregon Metallurgical, whereas the zirconium metallurgists were operating a bigger company but had no equity. Furthermore, the owner of Wah Chang had lived in New York and was thoroughly disliked, and now Teledyne, another absentee owner, would reap all the potential profits from zirconium. "Morale very bad in Albany" had festered for many years.

To sweeten morale a little in the meantime, I planned a new laboratory and office building and a general face lifting campaign. Steve cooperated passively. I was in touch with Singleton daily, and when he called, Steve always hopped up and left the office.

"Big doctor calling, eh?"

One day I asked, "Steve, why do you always refer to Henry as 'big doctor' and to George Roberts as 'number two doctor'?"

He said, "Very simple, Jim. George tries harder."

I thought things were settling down, but one day a representative of the United Steel Workers Union appeared and requested a conference. I found him an astute, affable, and capable union boss. Aware of the upheaval at Wah Chang, he was concerned about maintaining the same good relations with me that he had had with Yih, but at the same time he wanted to air some complaints from Yih's men and review their contracts with Teledyne. I thought that Steve had arranged, with his fine Chinese touch, to put on additional pressure.

Less than a week later, one of Wah Chang's largest customers called and said that the rumor was all over the industry that the Albany plant might be closed because of management problems. He requested an immediate meeting. This customer was very close to Yih. He was concerned because he had heard that Yih planned to set up a separate company to compete with Wah Chang. Since he was responsible for purchasing zirconium for his company, he needed to know the whole story. He encouraged me to accommodate Steve and thereby maintain plant production. Steve was putting on the heat.

Three weeks later I called one of the managers and found him absent. I called the second, also gone, then a third, with the same result. My secretary informed me that the twenty top managers were out on strike. She said that only Bill Walker, the personnel manager, had come to work.

"Well, get him over here."

When he arrived I said, "Bill, I understand that all the managers except you are out on strike."

"That's right, Mr. Nisbet."

"Why are you here?"

"Steve asked me to come," he said.

"Why? I thought you were all forming a solid front against Teledyne."

"That's right, Mr. Nisbet. It was discussed at Tops last night and we all agreed to strike in order to force our demand for an equity position, but they went out on their own. Steve is losing control of the management group."

"I don't like this. I am very aware of Yih's demands, as are Singleton and Roberts, and I think that with time we can accommodate all of you if you don't blow it with tactics like this. Give us more time."

"I really don't know what this strike is all about, Mr. Nisbet. Steve has been out of town and he hasn't given us any instructions. The management group is tired of waiting and we met privately to decide our own strategies. I am trying to go along with them, with you, and with what I think Steve wants. He called me last night and asked me to be here today. He felt that the plant could probably run for at least a while if I were here."

"Will the others be back tomorrow?"

"I don't know."

A few men returned the next day, and I assured them that if they continued to work I hoped to have a plan granting them an equity position very soon. At a subsequent meeting with the dissidents and Yih at Yih's home, I made the pitch that Teledyne was an honorable company and Singleton an honorable man, and that even though the equity commitment was not known to us before we acquired Wah Chang we were rapidly developing a plan to satisfy Li's and Oncken's long standing commitment. Finally, after debating with them for several hours, one of the managers broke the ice by saying:

"I believe Jim is sincere. I believe this is true of Teledyne, too. Let's go back to work, settle down, concentrate on producing zirconium, and await the equity ownership plan."

I thought at last the deadlock in this long, tedious intrigue was broken. We began the paper work immediately to set up the Albany operation as a separate company, granting the management group a ten percent equity position.

During my stay in Albany I had breakfast occasionally with Shelton, a close friend of Yih and the president of Oregon Metallurgical. Oregon Metallurgical was partially owned by Armco Steel. At one of the breakfasts I stumbled on a real scoop. Armco was negotiating with Steve to organize a new company to produce zirconium. Yih and his management group were offered 10% interest. Just after I learned this, we were stunned when Armco demanded an equity position in the Wah Chang plant. They thought they controlled Yih.

Shelton, who had interested the new ambitious chief executive officer of Armco in zirconium, acted as the liaison between him and Yih. Armco was eager to enter the zirconium business and I understood they had offered Yih the boss position, plus 10% of a new company, if Yih could bring his management group with him. This position to force an equity position in Wah Chang from Teledyne was highly developed, or alternatively, Yih would take his men to Armco.

Concluding that Armco had at least verbally arranged with Yih to buy our management group, I asked Shelton to tell Armco we were considering a $10 million suit against them for stealing the management of our company. Armco's aggressive attitude toward hiring Yih and his managers began to subside.

Yet we did stage a meeting with Armco in Portland. Frank LaHaye, a vice president from the corporate office, and I represented Teledyne. The financial vice president and an executive assistant to the president at Armco represented them. Steve Yih also attended. The question: would we sell Armco an equity position in Wah Chang, Albany?

The meeting lasted all day. The ideas discussed were poles apart. Finally, I offered Armco 20% of Wah Chang, Albany, for $20 million—a price I knew they would not pay. We departed. Frank and I went to Los Angeles to inform Henry and George of the outcome.

By the time the president of Armco called Singleton the following day it was confirmed that Singleton did not intend to sell anyone a position in Wah Chang at any price. Our meeting had been as successfully unproductive as Henry had wished.

I returned to Albany Saturday night. Sunday morning I went to Tops for breakfast. Steve Yih and Shelton were across the aisle and I joined them. Both had been in touch with Armco and knew the outcome of the Portland meeting.

I asked Steve to go back to the house with me to review the latest developments. After I applied all the pressure I could muster Yih finally agreed to call an executive at Armco and tell him that their jig was up. I got him promptly on the phone, and pressed him to stop this attempt to sabotage our operation. I told him that Yih was casting his lot with Teledyne. He doubted that, not knowing Yih was with me, and I put Steve on to tell him directly. Very subdued, he said:

"Steve here. What Jim says is right. My men are restless. We must settle down—make zirconium for Teledyne. Say hello to your president. Goodbye."

Chapter Twenty-Two

A HASSLE

When I got to my office the following Monday, Singleton called and asked me to get Steve to sign the new contract.

I said, "Henry, I know we discussed a new contract, but I did not know it had been finalized or presented to Steve."

"Oh yes, Steve has a copy of it."

"I haven't seen it myself yet."

"Steve has it. Get him to sign it. Let's solve this problem once and for all. When you returned to North Carolina a couple of weeks ago, Steve was in Los Angeles and George worked out a contract with him."

"O. K. As resident manager I am quite surprised. It's news to me."

Steve did, indeed, have a contract. The next morning he showed me pencilled notations on it indicating changes that he wanted. I had to read the contract hurriedly and after I called Henry, who agreed to Steve's changes, we had the contract re-typed and later that morning Steve signed it. This definitely called for a party.

At Steve's house that night there was a lot of conversation, much drinking and a good bit of noise—all problems solved, all wounds healed. Teledyne Wah Chang was accomplished in joint ownership.

After the party, I again went through Steve's contract and my initial shock was confirmed. Not only did Steve have an equity position in Wah Chang, Albany, but he also had a juicy option in Teledyne stock worth several hundred thousand dollars. I was particularly surprised because I had objected to the idea when George brought it up two months before. I thought I could have solved the problem without it.

I couldn't sleep that night. Early the next morning I called the corporate office. Neither George nor Henry had arrived.

I left word for Henry to call and decided to catch a plane

to North Carolina. The telephone rang before I left the house. Roberts and Singleton were on with profuse congratulations for a job well done.

I said, "The job well done has done me in with you. You negotiated separately with Yih. Granting him a cheap option for a bundle of Teledyne shares was too much. You know I advised against it, and why in hell not tell me?"

"Jim, you have been under considerable pressure," they consoled me. "Just relax and don't take it so seriously."

"Relax, hell!" I responded. "You should know better. I am returning to North Carolina today."

During the next several days I discussed the situation with my wife, Kay, and did not talk with Roberts or Singleton. My thinking crystallized. I saw then that the management group leaned toward Teledyne and away from Yih because, although they had great admiration and respect for him, they intuitively felt that he was overplaying his hand. Their unrest in turn had brought Yih into the fold, I thought. Roberts and Singleton, in negotiating the valuable option separately with Yih, had undermined my position.

I decided to resign. It was a matter of principle.

My wife Kay said, "I understand your point, but be sure you are resigning because of principle, rather than a badly punctured ego. You are expendable, but the Albany plant is not."

At my next meeting with George and Henry we had a heated argument. Finally, I beat the table and said:

"Henry, you have tainted our relationship."

I knew that contracts drawn in acquisition deals often favored an owner's position, but after this deal was made I violently objected to such management appeasement.

Following this row I went to Tokyo with Yih to negotiate a contract with a Japanese inventor for a new zirconium refining process. This gave me time to sort out in my mind my relations with Teledyne and to decide finally about resigning. I thought things had soured beyond my tolerance.

Part V
A PERSONAL TRAGEDY

Chapter Twenty-Three
CLOUDY WEATHER

"Lord, have mercy upon us
Christ, have mercy upon us
Lord, have mercy upon us"

When I returned from Tokyo to Los Angeles I did not visit the corporate office but instead met my wife Kay there. She had just completed her third cross country race as a participant in the Powder Puff Derby.

Kay had been enthusiastic about flying since I courted her by plane in 1945. After our four children were in school and Allvac prospered, she took flying instructions, quickly soloed, and got her private license and a Twin Comanche. She was an avid student of everything she undertook and kept advancing until she acquired an instrument rating and commercial pilot rating and was studying for an airline transport rating.

We flew home together across the fearful Rockies, the flat midwestern plains, and on to the eastern Blue Ridge Mountains. We had flown this route half a dozen times before and had often included the passages in Washington and Oregon, the Columbia River Basin, and between the snow-capped peaks of Hood, Shasta, Rainier, and Adams. On this trip, when we approached the Blue Ridge Mountains in Tennessee at 2 a.m. in dark, cloudy, menacing weather, we had to file an instrument flight plan from the air and soar through solid soup for three hundred miles. Then suddenly the clouds cleared away. Stars appeared and the moon brightened the cabin light. We were under the direction of Charlotte radar control and they called our plane, "Baron 477AP, Aero Plantation strip straight ahead—four miles."

I saw the dim lights on my back yard landing strip and the reflection from the moon on the nearby lakes looked like 100 acres of mirrors below. I responded to Charlotte control, "477AP—I have Aero Plantation in sight—cancel instrument flight plan." We landed and taxied to the security of home, where I had scarcely been for the prior three months.

137

A few days after our return Kay planned to fly to Danbury, Connecticut, to fetch back our boys' favorite teacher, Lee Ahlborn, and his wife from Kent School for a long weekend. I called about noon, just before she left, and asked if she had checked the weather. She said she had and it was O.K. going north, but later in the day there might be scattered cumuli nimbus buildups and thunderstorms on the return trip.

She flew to Danbury. When I arrived home at 6 p.m., Jack said that the Danbury airport operator had called for Kay to tell us she was off at 4:20 p.m. on an IFR flight plan and it would be solid soup all the way. Lee and Babs Ahlborn were with her. She would be in Charlotte about 7:30 p.m. At 7:15, I took off from Aero and monitored the Charlotte approach frequency. I planned to escort them to Aero Plantation. For thirty minutes I flew around but 477AP never checked in with Charlotte approach control. It was getting dark so I landed. Kay had said earlier that she would land at Charlotte rather than Aero if she arrived after dark. I asked the boys to drive to the Charlotte Airport to pick them up; that they must have been delayed by circumventing weather. I knew she hadn't landed to wait out a storm or she would have called. At nine o'clock, no word. At five minute intervals I was communicating by phone with the boys at Charlotte. No word. I thought to myself she must have landed, but I knew she had not. I thought she had to deviate miles around a storm but I knew by now her five hours of fuel would be depleted. An upsetting sense of despair gripped me.

The following transcription, provided to me by the Federal Aviation Agency, was recorded by the New York Flight Control Centers:

Kay to New York Control: "Baron 477AP off Danbury at 4:18 p.m. Climbing direct to Carmel."

New York Control: "477AP, radar contact. Cleared direct to Carmel. Climb to 8,000, report leaving 6,000."

A few minutes later Kay responded: "477AP at 6,000, on instruments in solid clouds."

New York Control: "477AP Roger. Change frequency to 126.8."

Kay on 126.8: "477AP at 8,000. Clouds broken, rising cumulus ahead. Slight turbulence."

New York Control: "Roger, radar contact."

Kay was approaching the busiest sector in the New York Control zone area. Weather was rapidly deteriorating. The ground controller in this sector was as busy as a cat trying to sort out incoming traffic from the west to the New York area. Other private pilots and airline captains vied for alternate clearances from the ground controller, and traffic was backing up west across Pennsylvania.

New York Control called a United Airlines captain: "United 483, hold at 12,000 over Lancaster."

United 483 responded: "Negative. My on board radar is painting severe weather over Lancaster. I am twenty miles west in the clear but can see a thunderstorm rising to 30,000 feet ahead. Request alternate position."

New York Control: "United 483, hold at present position. Wait further clearance; traffic backed up to Pittsburgh."

Another of many airlines in the Control Zone was Eastern. New York Control called Eastern: "Eastern 87, New York Control calling!"

The Eastern captain responded: "New York Control, don't talk to me now. I'm in severe turbulence in the middle of a storm and am headed out west at 270°."

A few minutes later Eastern called and reported a western course and requested a hold at Harrisburg at 10,000, which was granted.

Then a private pilot broke through the continuous radio chatter and the tone of his voice was dead serious:

"Cessna 310C to New York Control, at 6,000, 20 miles northeast of Lancaster. Severe turbulence. Request clearance for immediate descent to land."

New York Control: "Cessna 310C, cleared to descend to 3,000—await landing clearance."

At this time New York Control was well aware of the

storm over Lancaster, the flight path of Kay in 477AP, which had no on board radar.

New York Control: "477AP, are you O.K.?"

Kay: "477AP—I guess so. Solid soup, raining torrents, turbulent."

Then later, when Kay could break into the cluttered chatter, with a shaky voice she requested:

"477 A P — Re q st de vi ation 10⁰ lef t. Ex tr eme tur bu l ence."

New York Control: "477AP, 10⁰ left of course approved."

Kay didn't acknowledge and for five minutes New York Control called back to her with no response and finally suggested she change frequency to 122.6, Lancaster Flight Service. Then by telephone New York Control called Lancaster Flight Service and both frantically tried to contact 477AP.

Then minutes later Kay called New York Control:

"7 A P — R e que st fur th er de vi a tion 10⁰ l ef t."

New York Control: "477AP — deviation approved, radar contact lost, call Lancaster Flight Service on 122.6, 122.6. Do you read? 477AP — do you read New York?"

At home I was waiting. Kay was now overdue by two hours. I paced the floor and at ten minute intervals called Approach Control in Charlotte for word on 477AP. No word. Then the phone rang and I grabbed it—hoping—but sensing bad news.

* * *

"Mr. Nisbet?"

"Yes."

"This is the coroner in Lancaster, Pennsylvania. Baron 477AP cracked up in a severe thunderstorm over Lancaster, Pennsylvania. All three aboard were killed."

Holly cried. I called the boys at Charlotte and told them to come straight home; that their mother had landed at Lancaster, Pennsylvania. They sensed what had happened. I called Mary at a horseback riding camp in the mountains to come home. Brother Oliver and his wife walked in. They heard it from the sheriff's department. Thought I, too, was aboard 477AP.

Oliver and a pilot friend left early the next morning for Lancaster and returned about sunset. I met the plane. In the back was a plastic sack tied with a string. I shouted, "It couldn't be. It just couldn't be. My God! It can't be!"

Oliver hustled me away and the pilot took off for Atlanta for the cremation. The next day he returned with an urn of ashes in a velvet bag. The funeral followed two days later, and the ashes were interred at the family plot at old Waxhaw.

A few hundred people came to extend sympathy. I met them all with tranquilized and blurry eyes, and alone I walked at night in the woods and cried aloud beneath the pines and maples and oaks and pleaded to God for Kay's return—just for a day, only one day—please just one more day.

What now for the successful but heartbroken entrepreneur? Nothing, I suppose, but the lonely realization that the courage required to innovate was not solo, but derived in great measure from the courage and wisdom of Kay Nisbet.

I was deadened. Teledyne didn't matter. Nothing mattered. Kay, who had been with me at G.E., at Cyclops, at Allvac—the spirit of Allvac when I might have faltered—the intellectual crutch when I might have given in—the believer in me, now gone in a flash of lightning. The only therapy that exists, that of passing time, commenced.

For days afterward, or it seemed like weeks afterward, I turned in at eleven or twelve if the Scotch tasted good, and slept restlessly. At 1:00 or 2:00 a.m. each night the thunder roared and the lightning lighted my room and awoke me—a tumultuous thunderstorm to remind me of what? Kay was up in impossible wind shears, beyond the design of the Baron to handle. I'd think—"Why, God, do you emphasize the tragedy—what are you trying to tell me? It has happened—why remind me—why not let me sleep?"

A month later I soloed back to Los Angeles and admired the Rockies in contemplative solitude.

It was then that George and Henry first discussed with

me the idea of spending full time on acquisitions for Teledyne. My plan to resign faded with this new opportunity, judged from sadder and more mature eyes. My need then to plunge into continuous work and the challenge of acquiring for Teledyne prevailed.

I returned to Albany, Oregon, to see how the dust was settling at Wah Chang. The unusually capable group of managers, sparked by Yih, had returned to the business of running the company. A strong friendship between Yih and me had grown out of our trials and I had gained some understanding of the Oriental mind.

On this visit with Yih I asked, "Steve, what is the Oriental method of adjusting to tragedy?"

He replied, "Sorry, Jim, it's too late for you. The Oriental philosophy is 'Never get too closely attached'."

"Glad I didn't know before," I said. "Under that philosophy Kay and I would have missed too much."

Part VI
ACQUIRING COMPANIES FOR TELEDYNE

Chapter Twenty-Four

POUNDING THE AIRWAYS

"All changes–promotion, transfer, demotion, reorganization, merger, retirement, and most other managerial actions–produce loss. Despite the fact that change is necessary and often for the better, the new always displaces the old; and, at some level of consciousness, the individuals experience the stress of this displacement as loss." ... "Pain of Personal Management" ... Harvard Business Review– October, 1972

After the Wah Chang experience, I was spending more and more time on acquisitions and, thank goodness, less time with grubby old manufacturing companies.

Three weeks after Kay's accident the insurance company replaced my Baron with a new one. This was the third Baron I had had. I had flown Barons about 3,000 hours and felt quite at home on instruments even in the soup. I took off from Aero Plantation in late August of 1967 in pursuit of an acquisition in Toronto, Canada. The route took me slightly left of Lancaster, Pennsylvania, where Kay's crash had occurred. I was at 11,000 feet on top of scattered summertime clouds with distant cumuli nimbus rising to 20,000 feet far to the distant left and right—safe enough, but keeping my distance from these winds and thunderstorms of these monsters that take off a wing in a flash. I realized then it was my prosperity that allowed us "his" and "her" light twin engine planes in our planeport at home and that, in turn, was tragic.

I landed in Toronto and the new plane had functioned well except that the D.M.E. went out. Two days later I left Toronto about noon after filing an Instrument Flight Rules back to Charlotte. The weather was terrible: A 500 foot ceiling and raining torrents in Toronto and a 400 foot ceiling reported at Charlotte.

Just after takeoff and just before entering the soup my right door flew open and I circled and landed. The Baron door requires a delicate adjustment which this one hadn't had. In 15 or 20 minutes I was off again and on instruments in the soup and driving rain. Thirty minutes later I had reached altitude and leveled out at 9,000 feet over the middle of Lake Erie and the rain was very hard. Then I suffered the worst possible experience in an airplane—smoke and 15 seconds of loud static in my first radio which provides both voice and navigation communication. It went out. I said to myself, "Calm down—the plane is equipped with a duplicate set and it is functioning." Five minutes later the backup went out with a puff of smoke and a crackle. I'd lost all voice contact with the control centers and the major navigation aids. I was two hours from Charlotte with only a direction finder left. A 400 foot ceiling was last reported at Charlotte—too low to make an approach for landing with no voice. Besides, I didn't know within 30 or 40 miles where Charlotte was. Later on I was able to tune in WBT in Charlotte on the A.D.F. and cruised on wet with sweat, my mouth dry. I thought, "Lord, I believe you have it in for me and are punishing me beyond reason."

I cruised on and the rain finally lessened and the sky became brighter. About 100 miles out of Charlotte I broke out in the clear on top, with solid clouds beneath. I still didn't know whether the ceiling in Charlotte had lifted. Under such conditions the Instrument Flight Rules are to keep on destination according to the latest clearance, which was Charlotte. Twenty miles out a few breaks appeared in the clouds and I could see the ground. I knew I had at least 1,000 foot ceiling. Down I came and the Charlotte tower had a green light out for me to land. Ground control had followed me all the way on the transponder, which fortunately kept functioning. Later, I found out the windshield hadn't been properly sealed and my radios had shorted out with the rain. I went home but there was no one there for me to tell my latest flying experience.

* * *

In the fall of 1967 acquisition opportunities for Teledyne were mounting. Henry no longer had time to explore all the leads, even though a vice president, Bill Shannon, was working full-time with him on acquisitions.

The materials group of Teledyne grew to fifteen companies. In addition to the problems of integrating these companies into Teledyne, it was very difficult to instill in the older companies the aggressiveness and ambition for profit growth which was so necessary to Teledyne's internal growth. It was obvious to Singleton and me that my time would be better spent on acquisitions.

Henry and George asked me to give up the materials group and spend full time with Henry on acquisitions.

"O.K., Henry," I said. "What does the new job pay?" During my two years as vice president and materials group executive of Teledyne nothing was ever said about a raise. I had wondered about that and I wanted to find out if the new assignment was a promotion. I was rich at that time and it now occurred to me that I had not had a raise in two years.

Henry replied, "$80,000 per year."

This was a modest raise about equal to what I had earned at Allvac in 1961. I agreed, but wanted $100,000.

Bill Shannon and Henry were electronics oriented by experience and background. George Roberts was materials oriented, but by now he was pretty busy trying to run the operation of the Teledyne conglomerate. With the exception of Wah Chang, which I kept for a while, the companies in the materials group of Teledyne were split into three new groups, each with a new group executive. Thus the expansion of the corporate staff set in and each would soon take on a number of assistants.

It was clear to me that I could make acquisitions for 10 or 15 x E, with Teledyne stock at 40 to 50 x E, and contribute significantly to Teledyne's earnings per share. That was the name of the conglomerate game. I visualized bringing in a few million dollars per year to Teledyne's earnings, whereas the chance of that kind of growth in the combined materials companies was negligible. The companies that were growing tended to be the smaller ones and the companies that weren't growing, and in some cases were declining, the larger. The net growth from within was discouraging.

Henry must have had confidence in my acquisition judgment because he didn't even spend five minutes with me on acquisition policy. He asked me to work out of the corporate office in Los Angeles, but I did not want to move from North Carolina.

"O. K., live where you please," he said. "Spend some time in the Los Angeles office, keep in close touch by phone, and buy companies for Teledyne on the east coast."

"O. K.," I said, "But I'm tired of piloting my plane through icy winters and thunderstorm-splotched summers. Five years of that is enough. How about buying a jet and hiring a professional pilot? I feel like a gypsy in a different bed every night—alone." We talked it over and decided to hire a professional pilot and defer the jet.

Bill Shannon half emptied his acquisition prospects files and I set out on the acquisition trail. I had a busy and fascinating two years flying the East and acquiring companies for Teledyne.

Probably well over 50% of the companies Teledyne acquired were operated, controlled, and owned by entrepreneurs. The others were run by professional managers. It was always easier to acquire the entrepreneur because one individual usually had the authority to make a deal. Frequently a deal could be made with an entrepreneur in a day or two—sometimes only a few hours. These negotiations I enjoyed most. Consummating a deal was very satisfying.

It was not uncommon in dealing with a public company to get involved not only with the president and other officers, but frequently with an executive committee and a board of directors. Each would have a different slant, ranging from "my job" to "my shares", and including all gradations of interest between. Frequently we never got around to structuring an offer to some of the professionally managed companies, even after a half dozen visits. If a professional manager of a company does not want a deal, he is in a position to block it one way or another. I think he often fears—and it is probably justified—that new bosses will not be congenial.

Teledyne's acquisition strategy was probably typical of the good conglomerates, but quite different from old established companies that could not act as quickly. We would make an assessment of a company with respect to several factors:

(a) Is it profitable?
(b) Is the balance sheet good?

(c) Is the latest profit and loss (P & L) magnified in any way?

(d) Is the inventory clean?

(e) Is the backlog realistic and documented?

(f) Is management on top?

(g) Would management stay?

(h) Has there been a long range plan to maximize profits for a sellout?

(i) Does the business have growth potential?

(j) Can the profit grow?

(k) Can cash be drained from the company for application elsewhere?

(l) How is depreciation counted, and is it a significant percentage of profits?

Many of these questions could be answered from the Financial Statements but some required a jaundiced eye, and then the question boiled down to price.

For most of the companies we acquired during this period we paid 10 to 20 x E in Teledyne stock selling at 40 to 60 x E. In the early days Teledyne always paid stock for an acquisition rather than cash. There were two reasons for this: first, the stock price was rising rapidly and was therefore quite acceptable and second, at that time Teledyne did not have much cash. I made only two acquisitions for cash. One was a very small company for one-half million dollars and the other was a fairly large company whose president would not take stock. He seemed very stubborn to me at that time, but is probably worth more today. He refused $11 million in stock to accept $8 million in cash, and probably paid $2 million in taxes. But in the final analysis he was probably one of the shrewdest owners I acquired.

Each company acquired resulted in an immediate gain in Teledyne earnings per share. If they didn't grow, however, it was a one shot gain for that year. If the company acquired declined, as many did, it caused a subsequent downward drag in Teledyne's earnings per share. Looking back today, I think Teledyne would have been better off if we had acquired better growth companies, even though we would have had to pay 20 to 40 x E. The immediate gain would have been less, but the long range gain would have been continuing growth for Teledyne.

149

Chapter Twenty-Five

SOME COMPANIES WE BOUGHT-
SOME WE DIDN'T

When Teledyne acquired a Vasco subsidiary in Canada, it was changed to Teledyne—Canada. Cecil Franklin, Toronto entrepreneur who had owned M&J was elected as a director of Teledyne—Canada when his company was bought by George Roberts. Quickly following this Franklin heard about a successful company called Tank Truck which was run by a former truck driver, Lou Vettese. I went to Canada to join Franklin to negotiate a deal to merge Tank Truck with Teledyne—Canada.

Lou Vettese had formed Tank Truck twelve years before, starting with only the truck he drove. He was an experienced and capable truck driver and he understood other truck drivers as well as the business. Lou had other attributes, however. I learned in the three days spent with him in Toronto that he knew the maitre d's, waitresses, and members of the band at the prominent restaurants. Lou is a gregarious personality, in spite of his appearance. He is about 5'5", walks with a heavy limp, looks as though he has not slept in days, and has no pretenses about anything. He was attracted to the possibility of merging with Teledyne—Canada because the stock was traded daily on the Toronto exchange and he wanted to go public. He was aware that the price of Teledyne—Canada had advanced during the past year from $1 per share to $7 per share.

But the strongest reason was because his father, his silent partner, had developed a mania to have $1 million in cash. His father had some position in the company which was never made completely clear. I think the old man purchased the first truck Lou drove.

After two days of fascinating negotiations, Lou agreed to merge Tank Truck with Teledyne—Canada, and we fixed a price of $7 per share on Teledyne—Canada stock and offered him the equivalent of $5 million for his company. To us this was quite a buy, since Tank Truck had earned well in excess of $600,000 after taxes the prior year and was still growing.

So we shook hands and I sent our lawyer to Toronto to consummate the deal. Two weeks later I learned that the deal had been queered, so I returned to Canada. This session extended into the evening, and Lou danced with the singer in the orchestra, took her place as vocalist, and played the drums.

We discovered that Lou's father was hanging up the merger. He wanted one million dollars in his bank account in cash. Pop was not a stockholder at Tank Truck, but Lou was determined to accommodate him because of that first truck.

The following day we persuaded a Toronto bank to loan Lou one million dollars on the stock he was to receive. The acquisition was accomplished only after this peculiar deference to the old man.

This acquisition increased the Teledyne—Canada earnings substantially and the stock rose rapidly to $17 per share within six months. With the strong Teledyne—Canada price we were able to make several more acquisitions of small companies in Canada.

* * *

Remember Firth Sterling, the special steel company that was a big Allvac customer while it copied Allvac's vacuum melting facilities? I made a few passes at acquiring Firth Sterling for Teledyne and decided the company was not good enough. George later bought it anyway at a high price and in spite of my repeated advice that he not do so. In the meantime, the Firth Sterling high temperature alloy and tool steel business was liquidated or partially picked up by Vasco and Allvac. Teledyne is now struggling to keep Firth Sterling afloat as a separate company in the tungsten carbide business. It was that business that George wanted so badly, but unfortunately the plant is located in the industrial dungeons of McKeesport, whose climate is about as viable as the old four-story textile plants left beside the rivers and creeks in New England. The carbide business should have been started fresh, either in a cotton field in Carolina or a wheat field in Kansas.

* * *

We were introduced by a company finder to a small company in the aluminum business. Its manufacturing operations involved a complex metallurgical process. I spent a day in their manufacturing plant and met all the manufacturing management personnel. Then I conferred with the president at the company's corporate offices and met the other officers. I was ready to conclude that the price of this company might be in excess of ten times earnings because of its higher than average technical complexity and potential growth. During the latter part of my visit with the president when we were sparring about the price, I commented:

"I have spent two days with you and your men, and I have seen your plant and observed the complexity of your technical operation, but I do not recall meeting anyone that you specifically identified as a metallurgist or an engineer. We are interested in companies based on technology, and your operation certainly is metallurgically complex. I must have missed the chief metallurgist and the chief engineer."

I was suspicious that their future technology might have been dropped and recent earnings maximized.

The president said, "Mr. Nisbet, we had several metallurgists here when we were first getting this complex technical operation underway. At that time, it was operated as a laboratory, or at best as a semi-production pilot plant. You understand. We found a great deal of difficulty in finally reducing it to a routinely operating business. Finally, to accomplish this, we had to fire our metallurgists and engineers. We found that they interfered with production."

We passed up this company but it was acquired later by a competitive conglomerate. Quite recently they spun it off again—I suspect because they found a void in its technical content and serious problems in the inventory values. It was a case of a company being set-up to be sold.

* * *

Another company Teledyne did not acquire was a finance company in Michigan that did a factoring business and made consumer loans—a "respectable" loan shark. A year before negotiations, Teledyne had acquired some finance and insurance companies, and Henry Singleton liked the financial flavor.

We had heard about the company from two sources. One was a gentleman who presented himself as a finder and wanted first to negotiate a couple hundred thousand dollars in finder's fees if the deal went through. Simultaneously, we heard of the desire of the company to have discussions with Teledyne directly. It developed later that the so-called finder was not only a major stockholder but also on the board of directors. We kept up a finder's fee sparring match with him while the negotiations went forward.

Henry joined me in these negotiations and we had a five hour session with three members of the executive committee. Henry hypnotized them with his knowledge of finance and business and with the virtue of Teledyne. During the next few weeks I had several conversations with members of the company board and particularly with one board member who seemed to be the key influence. We thought we had the price settled and a deal looked promising. The so-called "finder director" kept trying to reconstruct the finder's fee but nobody paid much attention to him.

The president of the company was one of the largest stockholders. But, as one would not expect, he was given the title of president and paid a handsome salary in exchange for an understanding that he would not exercise any of the authority or responsibility of president, but would subordinate his role to those of the chairman and executive vice president. The president realized that he would not last as president after the merger papers were signed, so I negotiated separately with him for his future and readily agreed to continue to pay him for five years—if he agreed not to work.

Ten days later, Henry and I had a second all day session with the executive committee and about half of the twenty-five man board. Bargaining again went well except that a shrewd lawyer and board member from Philadelphia was present. He challenged Henry several times during the meeting and scowled when Henry was at his best expounding the virtues of Teledyne. After Henry and I had excused ourselves to talk outside the meeting about the deal, we finally met what we thought was their price. I fully expected the tough lawyer, who literally thought Teledyne stock was Chinese money, to shout "Bull!", but he restrained himself.

Two weeks later the executive committee fooled us by unanimously rejecting the Teledyne offer. We were shocked. It was a big deal and a big disappointment.

Henry said to me later, "Well, Jim, we didn't waste much time on it, so let's not fret any further about it." And then he shrewdly added, "Perhaps we should have offered them 10% more than they asked just an hour before their meeting. Then the majority of the owners on the board would have smothered that Philadelphia lawyer."

Chapter Twenty-Six

COMPETITIVE ACQUIRERS

Teledyne's speed in assessing an acquisition is illustrated by the case of a small $5 million electronics company. Shortly after I heard about this company I learned that a friend at a billion dollar blue chip company was interested. I told him we would be in competition, and I promptly pursued negotiations by calling the president of the electronics company that day and talking with him for an hour. I determined that the president was also the founder and owner. He had operated the company at no profit for five years. His plan was to sell out at a price considerably in excess of his investment and he didn't plan to be profitable in the future. He wasn't a business man. At Teledyne this information is sufficient for us to pass, as I did at the end of the phone conversation. Opportunities might be missed by making such quick decisions but we didn't gamble on inventors. My friend called six or eight weeks later and said he was now ready to negotiate with the electronics company. He had finally gotten it cleared through his hierarchy. By then I had forgotten about it, but I suggested to him that he pursue it with all deliberate speed.

The conglomerate technique of rapid acquiring was possible because we had no corporate clearance maze. Modern conglomerates had competition only from other modern conglomerates in the acquisition parade and none could act faster or more decisively than Teledyne.

Another company we did not buy was an over-the-counter company in Virginia. I had known about it since it was organized in 1960. The company was in the plastics business and represented a growing opportunity, but since its inception it had had several sets of management before finally returning a profit. The over-the-counter price was 3—3¼ when I was invited by the company to discuss merging with Teledyne.

I revisited the manufacturing operation and had several sessions with the management, particularly with the absentee chairman. The company had earned 20c per share in the previous year, but with management difficulties I thought their value was less than $2 a share. With the public price in excess of $3, there was no point in further negotiations. But another "wild" conglomerate came on the scene and, after a cursory and superficial study of the company, offered them $4 per share in stock. In addition to that, they guaranteed the $4 price equivalent in the public value of their shares for one year into the future—a deadly deal. Deals that guarantee the future price of stock are pure folly and, as far as I know, at Teledyne we never practiced such business. The deal for the plastics comany made by this competitor was in 1969, and at the peak in their public stock value. Before the year ended, the number of added shares paid out by that conglomerate was equal to the number of original shares.

The prospectus issued by this acquirer at the time of this deal showed eight acquisitions pending, and seven of the eight involved similar deals with future stock price guarantees. A year later this conglomerate had a huge deficit, as they should have. In 1969 more and more of this kind of action by the marginal conglomerate companies signaled the financial recklessness that the acquisition parade had reached. It was an early warning that conglomeration would soon come to an end.

Today, six years later, this same little plastics company and many others that the reckless conglomerate acquired have been spun off. In the case of this conglomerate, deconglomerization had to set in, and probably 50% of the companies it acquired during the past six or seven years will have to be spun off to hold the conglomerate together. However, they can only sell off their good companies and give away their bad ones, so their future is bleak.

Chapter Twenty-Seven

SOME OWNERS ARE PLEASED-MANY NOT

I have talked with several owners and managers of companies Teledyne bought, and I had hoped to cite a few examples of pleased and enthusiastic sellers, but I have found that most of them have departed. They were pleased with their stock, but now the value had gone to pot.

The reaction of entrepreneurs who sold companies to Teledyne was sometimes complete disenchantment. Since these people were often the outspoken type, it was sometimes expressed in print. I don't entirely agree with the following example but it is a strong man's strong opinions.

"Paul Keller Going Back Into Business—at Age 66"...American Metal Market, January 8, 1971.

Over a period of 20 years or so he built his Osco steel warehouse business into a highly successful independent $15,000,000 a year enterprise.

Then in 1968 he sold out to a conglomerate.

Lonesome Years

"These have been the lonesomest three years of my life," he says.

He has come to feel that conglomerates have let everybody down—the customers, the suppliers and the employees.

"They eliminate humanity. They're cold blooded, dollar-oriented Frankensteins," he says vehemently. "I don't like the principle on which they operate."

No Community Interest

"The people who helped build these companies had a home and a civic pride. This is being totally destroyed as the financial pools supporting the conglomerates have no interest in the communities as such."

What was wrong with being part of a conglomer-

ate? Practically everything according to ex-entrepreneurs like Mr. Keller.

Can't Run Business

"They assure the former owners they can continue to run their businesses. But the owners find they can't; the real rules are made by an absentee owner.

"They send in a personality boy who does the negotiating, then the lawyers come out and write up a lot of stuff that puts you in a still different ball game. From then on," says Mr. Keller, "you follow the financial people and the hatchet people sent out from heaven knows where."

I had been the negotiator for Teledyne when Osco Steel was acquired. After reading this blast, I could not resist writing to Paul. For the first time in my life I had been accused of being a "personality boy." He did not answer my letter.

Chapter Twenty-Eight

THE CLIMATE CHANGED

In 1969 financial writers began referring to high multiple conglomerate stocks as Chinese money and conglomerate acquisitions as a chain letter business.

The founders of conglomerates were sensitive and always tried to deny the name. Integon once advertised the most ridiculous denial of all: "Integon is not a conglomerate, but rather a congeneric, a conglomerate with discipline."

A few companies continued desperately to acquire but frequently with a negative effect on earnings per share. This method never did fit the "sensible" conglomerate formula.

In June of 1970, after the Teledyne stock price collapsed and acquisitions subsided, I travelled to the corporate office in Los Angeles to take new soundings in the light of a new climate. At a meeting with Singleton in his plush twentieth floor office on the Avenue of the Stars we discussed the death of acquisitions. I had not been able to make a deal to acquire a company in three or four months. The gap in multiples between the acquired and the acquirer had reversed.

The Los Angeles Country Club lay beneath us, trim and lush with manicured greens, white sand traps, and palms bordering neat fairways. I introduced the subject of my recent idleness and reminded him that I had cut expenses by letting my pilot go, again flying the airways by myself. He reflected on this, his blue eyes clear, and on one of those rare occasions in my experience with him, he reminisced:

"Remember, Jim, the fascinating experience we had after acquiring Wah Chang?"

"Why don't you continue to pay me, Henry, and commission me to write the story?" I asked.

Henry resorted to a tactic he frequently employs and changed the subject, "I never thought about that." And then he quickly followed with his first compliment to me, which carried with it a grave note:

"Teledyne recognizes your great success and your past contributions."

"Past, Henry?"

He changed the subject again and called George Roberts on the intercom and said:

"Jim is here. Could you join us for lunch?"

George came into the office and Henry asked, "Do you have anything in mind that we could dream up for Jim to do?"

I couldn't understand Singleton's casual attitude toward me, one of his officers who thought he had been diligent and had contributed a great deal to the success of Teledyne.

George looked out the window and was silent longer than normal. Then he rambled:

"Well, Jim, you know the materials group which you headed prior to working directly with Henry is now split three ways with three group executives."

I replied, "I realize that, but we all know that the reorganization and shake-down of Teledyne must continue. It's a new organization and must always change like a growing organism. Companies with completely diverse policies, procedures, and modus operandi must be assimilated together. We have discussed the possibility of three executive vice presidents instead of the splintered set-up with several vice presidents and a dozen group executives. This kind of organization is needed and I have tried to get this idea on the table for several years."

He said, "You might be interested in consulting for the next three or four years. We have done that in many cases, as you know, with owners and managers of companies who have left for various reasons. They are now consultants at $10,000 annually."

I realized now that I was teetering just off the top rung of the Teledyne management ladder and my footing there was insecure. I had concentrated on buying companies for the past three years and now acquisitions had dried up. In the meantime, George Roberts had been scrambling to absorb the new companies as they were folded into Teledyne ownership. He shuffled them under this or that group executive and tried to deal with the inevitable awkwardness of managing and controlling them. Teledyne "Corporate" was too young to have developed a professional philosophy or esprit de corps to absorb the influx of foreign cells. For example, during the five years that I was a vice president of Teledyne I never attended a single meeting in Henry's office when there was anyone else present except, occasionally, Roberts, and it was almost the same when I was materials group executive and met with Roberts. From my vantage point Teledyne "Corporate" didn't exist in terms of group management but was directly controlled and directed by "King" Singleton through Roberts.

I was getting into a box I was not prepared for. The prospect of my $100,000 standard of living being adjusted to $10,000 forthwith was unpalatable. I suggested that we go to lunch.

Lunch was pleasant at the Los Angeles Country Club. We discussed various companies in Teledyne, reminisced about this and that, and speculated to some extent about the future. Returning to the office, I thought my best strategy would be to depart quickly.

"I'll return to North Carolina to think about what we have discussed," I said. "We can communicate by phone, or I could return within the next few weeks."

And I left.

Nothing happened for four or five weeks. I learned first hand about the silent treatment for executive execution. And they controlled "my" company, Allvac, the best cell in Teledyne.

At the end of the month I called Henry for a date to return to Los Angeles. Henry was always readily available to me by phone. I do not recall ever having communicated with his office, almost a daily occurrence for two years, when he was not available by phone wherever he was. He told me to come out the following day. My resignation was then imminent.

Roberts was out of town. I had a long conversation with Henry. I think he received one telephone call. His telephone conversations are short, except those he initiates when he is courting a reluctant suitor. He spends his time thinking and reading books, and is not interested in chit-chat. He is interested in grappling with major intellectual, technical, and financial matters—like *The World History of Interest Rates*, which he was reading that day.

I said, "Nothing has been suggested that I am interested in pursuing further as an officer of the company. I assume, perhaps I'm presumptuous, that you and George could cook up something to keep me so-called 'gainfully employed', but that idea is distasteful to me. I am resigning as an officer effective today and hope to be well-paid as a consultant for three years. Finally, sell me back my Baron plane at book value."

Singleton heard me clearly and on the back of a scratch pad wrote down what I had said. Henry bought multimillion dollar companies on scratch pads.

"That's a little steep, Jim."

"Perhaps it is, Henry, but remember 'my great past services'."

"Yes, I remember. It's all right. O. K., I'll agree."

He gave me a Xerox copy of the three line scratch pad deal and we shook hands. That was my three year contract.

"I'm available any time you want me, Henry, for three years."

The three years ended with not one call for consultation. The three-year contract was really an agreement not to work and not to bother Singleton.

But the fact is, Singleton has no problem in making up his own mind in running Teledyne. He is the king. The decisions he reaches are well transmitted down through the charisma of Roberts and contradictory opinions by the professional division managers are filtered out before being filtered up.

I returned to Charlotte in June 1970, not as vice president of Teledyne, but as consultant to Teledyne in name only. The following day I called my broker and, except for option-plan stock, sold all my remaining Teledyne shares at $35 to $40/share. I had been reluctant to sell all prior to this, even though I was nervous about the declining price. Loyalty and sentimentalism deterred me, and cost me several hundred thousand dollars. Two years before the price was $70/share but two years later it hit a low of $9.50/share. $40/share for Teledyne stock would be equivalent to $20/share for Allvac.

Perhaps Henry's conscience was beginning to hurt him. He realized that he was having a difficult time keeping the entrepreneurs that ran growth companies that Teledyne had acquired. Perhaps he hoped that we might feel kindly toward him in the future as we grew older and sought new businesses to conquer without pensions in spite of long careers in the corporate world.

Although for several years I was listed as the third highest paid officer of Teledyne, I never felt quite at home there. I never felt that the corporate footing was sound.

Teledyne lacked the great tradition of G. E. where I had worked for sixteen years. Nothing could match the great excitement I had in creating Allvac metals, yet my employment at Teledyne was very exciting and fulfilling in many ways, though frustrating at times because I again had bosses.

* * *

About this time my personal life was rejuvenated when I married the belle of New Canaan, Connecticut—Margy Hazard. Not being imbued in Allvac and Teledyne history, she took it all very casually, and that helped me sever my ties with the company.

So I retired for a month to contemplate my future.

I was programmed by Puritan Presbyterian work ethic at birth. If I am idle my conscience hurts.

Summering in Rhode Island, playing golf every morning, sitting on the beach every afternoon, and drinking cocktails at night—the very idea of being retired was not my cup of tea.

Besides, my handicap did not improve at all.

Part VII

SEARCHING FOR AN ENCORE

The nice thing about being a private investor is that one's mistakes can be kept private, but having been open up to this point in this treatise I must be consistent to the end and admit other mistakes in this realm too.

Chapter Twenty-Nine
VENTURE CAPITAL

*"To exist is to change, to change is to mature, and to
mature is to go on creating one's self endlessly." . . .*
                                        Henri Bergson

As we grow older we reach new ages of understanding.
For example: gallstones, bursitis, and golf scores in the 90s;
seven children now about formally educated and seeking
their individual niches. Carol had our first grandchild; Jim,
Jr., wrote a novel and doesn't own a suit; Jack is a naturalist
watching birds; Mary raising Afghan dogs; John running
his freighter in the Mediterranean—an entrepreneur; Rick
and Holly have another year in college with wholesome
outlooks and love affairs; Jim and Margy adjusting to an
empty house.

But that is backward looking. I'd rather go forward and
pursue new business ventures. I didn't like living off my
capital and seeing it decline. I didn't want to go back to a
routine job, even if I could find one. But I like a high standard of living and even if I didn't, Margy does.

I experienced substantial financial losses in resigning
from Teledyne: life insurance, a stock option, a pension at
65, a comfortable salary—and I was too young for Social
Security.

But the greatest loss was not having daily responsibility which I had grown accustomed to and enjoyed for
thirty-odd years. Again I had arrived at a crossroad. I must
search for an encore in business.

So on I went thrashing around in the business world.
Private investing and managing money is a quite different
discipline than managing a business.

My interest as a private investor naturally falls into the
three areas related to my past experiences: (1) I'd like to
sponsor young entrepreneurs who have a burning desire to
create a new business. (2) I believe I should be smart enough
to invest successfully in new growth companies with proven
track records and hope to avoid being whip-sawed in the bull

and bear markets when values swing from 1 to 5 and back from 5 to 1. Finally, (3) my land should be developed. Those are the businesses I have evolved in my mind to be pursued.

Venture investing sometimes leads into unexpected places. Harry Dalton, the former Allvac director mentioned earlier, in addition to his many other interests is an art collector. On the wall in his office he had an unusually attractive nude picture painted by Capuletti, a famous Spanish artist. For five years I tried to persuade Harry to sell me that picture. Finally, I offered him 1,000 shares of a little chemical company in which we were both directors. I had paid $1.00 per share for the stock and it was worth at least $3.00 at that time. Harry finally agreed to trade. The little chemical company has since done very well, and the stock has traded recently at $20. Now, every time I look at my beautiful nude picture, I can only think of her as a $20,000 broad.

It has been pointed out by many venture capitalists that new ventures fail more often than they succeed, even though up front both the man and idea appear to be "A+." Also, it's wiser to invest in an "A" rated man and a "B" rated idea than in a "B" man and an "A" idea. With this thesis in mind I ventured forth with some capital and searched for "A" ideas and "A" entrepreneurs. A few examples, some with short lives, follow:

A 45 year old chemist appeared with an idea for reprocessing chemicals that could no longer be dumped into streams; a good idea ("A") because tons of the stuff had been indiscriminately dumped in the creeks before Environmental Protection Agency said "no." I thought the chemist at 45 was a little too old and he didn't have such a great track record, but he was a good salesman and seemed to know the technology. I'll admit stretching it a little to rate him "A-". A friend joined me and we put up $15,000 each for common stock with rigid rules requiring monthly financial statements. In six months the little company was broke and couldn't meet its small payroll and we were yet to receive the first financial statement.

The fast talking chemist salesman who organized it talked a bank into a large loan with the equipment as collateral. When the company repeatedly failed to meet payments the bank foreclosed. I hurried out to the plant when I heard the bad news. While chatting with the jolly president I noticed someone in a blue business suit twenty feet up on top of a chemical processing tower wiping off pipes with a dirty rag. I asked the failed entrepreneur, "Who is the dressed-up stranger on the tower?" The jolly president laughed and said, "He is the banker looking for a serial number on the equipment for his foreclosure papers." The pain of failure didn't dampen the entrepreneur's sense of humor.

Pollution control became a popular subject for new businesses in 1972 and I invested in two others that year. One went public at a very high price and I sold out at a good profit—30 x—and the other I sold to a partner when we separated.

Four years ago I invested $128,000 for controlling interest in a company which assembles and distributes bucket trucks and digger derricks and related equipment to power companies and telephone companies. Although the product is not glamorous I was impressed with their history of growing earnings. The president, Doc Query, is a great salesman and knew the business—"A+". This will never be a bonanza but a modest income producer. This type of investment is far less risky than a start-up. In this case there was a five year record of growth and earnings, but the chances for a multifold increase in value is not there either. The business idea should rate about "C".

Another one I'm stuck with is a substantial investment in a vacation prefab house company. It is dead broke and can hardly pay its telephone bill and I must mentally classify it as a write-off.

There were a few other so-so companies but I still search for the venturesome dream—$1 invested equalling $10 in five years. I am looking for another Allvac.

My interest in a real estate development was not exactly planned. In 1960 I bought 500 acres ten miles from Charlotte and built myself a posh home, a private landing strip, seventy acres of man made lakes and a nine hole golf course. Other people happened along who shared my interest in this type of country living. I divided the place into 108 large lots and have sold off 35 of them to others. People also came who liked my houses, so I sold several of them and built for myself the "Rembrandt" of all that someone will want to buy soon. I'm a frustrated architect and like to design and build houses. From an investment viewpoint this has been a capital sink-hole because the cost of the lakes, the strip, the golf course, the tennis courts and seven miles of private roads has been very high. But who knows? I might someday recoup the development cost and make a million on the land venture. But with prices at $7,000 to $10,000 per acre the lots sell ever so slowly.

One of my investments was a start-up situation and it is probably typical of so many new companies—the trials and tribulations, running out of capital, very frayed nerves, almost quitting several times along the way—learning fast from the forces of the markets and responding too slowly, but finally seeing the light one day. I elaborate on this one in the following pages and update it later. It ties in with my interest in growth companies.

Both my interest in sponsoring young entrepreneurs with venture capital and my interest in investing in growth companies came together when I met two bright young PH.D's who had indeed devised a sophisticated, scientific system for investing in growth companies. Their system was consistent with my own general ideas but had been developed to a scientific degree. It also worked with real money invested in the market. That is the true test. I thought I'd found a great opportunity to sponsor a new venture capital company and at the same time had found a systematic and scientific way to invest in the stock market.

For several years, while employed by DuPont, Phil Manning and John Fogle had moonlighted nights and weekends developing this system. A computer was necessary to accomplish the myriad calculations the system required. With real dollars invested their performance record was superb even in the bear market of 1970. It showed a compounded growth rate of better than 30%. I was very enthusiastic. This was exactly my idea of an interesting and potentially rewarding approach to investing. I took my new-found friends home with me to spend the night and the next day I made a deal to provide the venture capital they required to shake them loose from DuPont and move them to Charlotte.

172

The agreement I made was simple. We set up a 3-way money management partnership and I agreed to put in the seed capital to be managed and also agreed to help bring in additional capital through outside limited partners. My contract required that I obligate myself to advance up to $100,000 to pay their salaries for a three year start-up period and the advance would be paid back from future partnership profits.

At this time I was associated with Olin Nisbet, III, in other management partnerships and accounts which Olin managed by the intuitive method. The two methods, "scientific" and "intuitive," didn't fare well together and after about one year of antagonism between the two they had to be separated and I had to choose between them. Olin returned with his accounts to Interstate Securities (the brokerage house that his late father and Allvac Director, Olin Nisbet, Jr., had founded in 1930). At the time we separated we split the $5 million we had under management. Olin, III, like his father, is a very shrewd young man and has since been very successful. I stuck with the scientists, Phil and John, and in another year with more limited partners and good market conditions we grew up to about $5 million under management—the systematic approach worked, at least at first. Every week we counted our paper profits and gloated about our "smarts" in the market.

A short time after Phil and John moved to Charlotte in January, 1971, I asked Phil this question:

"What are the twenty best growth companies on the American and New York stock exchanges today? Where are the young 'Allvacs' or the new 'Teledynes'? Might we find a 'Xerox'?"

Phil Manning, being an unusually decisive fellow, said:

"Here are the Annual Reports of the twenty best growth companies today, but don't assume these twenty will be the best tomorrow. They fade with time."

"But Phil," I asked, "why do you have Annual Reports? You say you follow only earnings per share and the price action and never read Annual Reports."

Again Phil had a ready answer: "Don't misunderstand me, Jim. I don't read Annual Reports. I am not impressed by the presidents of these companies bragging about their ambitious expectations for the future. I have the Reports because these are the twenty best listed growth companies with oustanding historical growth records, a huge following in the market, and strong and rising stock prices. We own these stocks and they send us their Annual Reports."

I said, "Phil, you know I am very leery of stocks that sell over 30 to 40 x E. What is the P/E ratio of your selected list of twenty?"

"You have impressed us with your preoccupation with high multiple stocks," Phil answered. "I checked this list recently. The average P/E ratio is 37. How about that?"

"Rather expensive," I said. "I have had experience in the high multiple period of both Allvac and Teledyne. One day at Allvac I was a high multiple stock millionaire and then quickly the change in the multiple changed my position to a non-millionaire. I went through that same rise and fall with Teledyne stock. Does your system avoid the fall? When these companies' earnings growth falters, their prices will fall a hell of a lot faster than they rose."

One of the twenty best companies was Levitz. When Levitz common stock reached a price of $90 and was approaching 100 x E, I rushed to Phil Manning's office and suggested that he sell Levitz. Phil said:

"To sell would be a violation of the system, and according to our agreement the system must be inviolate."

I had to agree but went away thinking that Levitz was grossly overpriced. During the next two months the price of Levitz common stock rose to $150. Again I nervously approached Phil and suggested that perhaps our rules should be revised to include an automatic sell signal if the price earnings ratio exceeded 100. I admitted that I was wrong when I first suggested selling at $90 but surely I was right in recommending that he sell at $150. Again Phil patiently explained, "I will get a signal when there is weakness in the stock price so stop fretting. Besides, Jim, I bought the stock at $20."

The following week distressing articles on Levitz Furniture appeared in *Barrons, Forbes,* and *The Wall Street Journal.* The authors, doubting as I was, could not stand such a high multiple on any stock.

Trading in Levitz was stopped for a few days after reaching a high of $150. It reopened at $135 and immediately rose back to $155. Then the stock split three for one and soared to $60. At that time the SEC decided that the latest prospectus to sell 600,000 shares was incomplete and the New York Stock Exchange again stopped trading. When reopened in June, 1972, Levitz was $35. We have since sold it at $38 per share because of this poor price action in relation to the market as a whole, probably the early warning signal that the tide of earnings growth might be ready to fade. Levitz, like Teledyne before, was growing so fast that, if continued at that rate, it would soon have been the only furniture distributor left in the world. We know that can't happen. Therefore, Levitz faces the huge problem of controlling its transition from a growth company with an astronomical growth rate of better than 50% per year for six years to a mature company. In some sweet year earnings will be lower than the year before and then the price earnings ratio will plunge.

Levitz did falter and the price of the stock has since continued down. Recently the quarterly earnings per share were up only 1c. The price action for the prior period of three to four months had anticipated that poor earnings report. I'm glad we sold at $38. In July, 1973, Levitz was $5. The truth frequently leaks out and the stock price falls before it is reported in print in *Barrons, Forbes,* or *The Wall Street Journal.*

In Figure 2 a band shows the boundaries of earnings per share for a ten year period for the twenty companies. The earnings growth curves all fall within the shaded band, between a 50% and a 20% compounded growth rate. This band is well above our basic criteria of selection (i.e., a 15% compounded growth rate for four years). The twenty best of the two hundred companies followed are selected on the basis of their price growth action and in most markets the best action occurs in companies whose compounded growth rate exceeds 20% per year. These companies also tend to sell at the highest earnings multiple, frequently at 30 or 40 x E and sometimes even higher.

Superimposed on the band of the twenty select growth companies are the great growth records for Litton, Xerox, and Teledyne. The Litton curve shows the demise of Litton when it fell from the grace of growth in 1968. Coincident with this, the price earnings ratio for Litton dropped from 60 x E to 7 x E. Shortly afterward, the growth rate of Teledyne subsided with similar results.

Xerox continues to grow and continues to sell at a multiple near 50. The rate of growth, however, even in the classic Xerox, is tapering off. A few years hence, or it could be a few months or even tomorrow, it is inevitable that more and eventually all of the twenty select growth companies of 1972 will fall from grace and their multiples will tumble, in the fashion of Litton and Teledyne when earnings growth faltered. Or if the general market turns from bullish to bearish the P/E ratio will fall. The average P/E ratio for growth companies ranges between 20 and 40, depending on the market.

This reminds me of a question I put to Henry Singleton before we merged Vasco. "With the sales growth of Teledyne so phenomenally steep, isn't our future problem to control maturity and perhaps slow the present pace by buying real growth companies at 30 x E rather than dogs at 10 x E?"

As this book was reaching completion early in 1973 we were witnessing a bear market and the average P/E multiple of the growth stock index was continuing its downward trend. At the moment we were completely out of the market and had our partners' cash stashed away in bank certificates of deposits. We were waiting and ready to invest again in the newer growth companies at high multiples when the bulls return to Wall Street. Several of the "select" list of twenty in 1972 have already disappeared and new ones will be added for the next bull market. The story of this venture in the systematic method for investing and losing money was just beginning.

The Nisbet-Manning-Fogle partnership entered into several years ago with such great expectations passed through the valley of death and the brink of failure. It

GROWTH COMPANIES

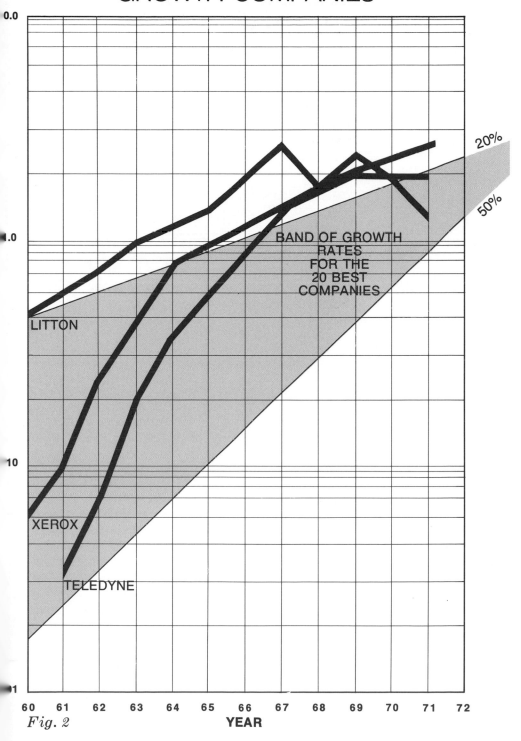

Fig. 2

YEAR

177

finally emerged in a completely new and different direction, in addition to its original forte of managing money with a computer program. It now appears to be one of those rare finds in the venture capital business that might be a ten-fold gain in the next five years. The partnership was originally set up to manage capital by sophisticated methods, computer programmed, based on models of historical stock market price trends—a system devised to beat the market.

The partnership spent a very successful two years in the management of partners' funds that grew to about $5 million. Then the stock market hit the skids in 1973 and the system's "sell signals" didn't work quickly enough. I came into the office one morning and Phil Manning told me we had a drop of 7% in the value of our market investments the day before. The system was designed on a weekly input/output basis and it took the computer two to four weeks to develop strong buy or sell signals. A few weeks later the computer was shouting "sell, sell, sell." The debacle was compounded by the fact that we held very heavy investment positions in small, thinly traded growth stocks. So when we started to sell 10,000 shares of Pizza Hut or Sambo's Restaurants we had to take a real "bath" in the rapidly declining market. This proved what I always suspected—that there is no perfect system to beat the market consistently.

With the combination of losses from the rapidly falling market prices and the limited partners' capital withdrawals, the $5 million we had invested rapidly declined to $2.5 million and my own liquidity was about wiped out. Even so I was obligated under the contract with my partners to continue to add more capital to the business and I did up to $100,000.

This was a venture where I would rate the two young partners "A" each, but their idea of managing money in the stock market by a computer program now had to be rated "B" or "C". But that isn't too bad because there is no such thing as an "A" market system that has any longevity. It was great in a bull market but bad in a rapidly developing bear market. My additional capital was soon consumed and Phil and John had to take out second mortgages on their homes for the partnership to survive. This created anger in their wives which took several weeks and longer to settle down. They didn't understand nor believe that the Capital Angel had also to mortgage his house to survive his liquidity crunch.

We had a series of survival meetings and decided that the computer software talent and expertise was still there and that talent must be focussed in new directions fast. The two great years of managing money with a computer program were damaged in two short months and restructuring that business any time soon with more new partners and that track record was too dismal even to contemplate. We had to turn elsewhere and find new applications for their expertise. I gave them a contract to automate the bookkeeping and inventory control systems at Utilities Services Inc., another of my venture capital companies. I called my old friend, Ed Gaskins, of the American Bank & Trust Company in Monroe, and pleaded our case and their brilliance in the software realm. Ed kindly signed a contract to develop a software program for his mortgage department.

With the residual income from the investment management business and the two new contracts our expenses still exceeded income by $3,000 a month. The pressure was on to develop more business or die. An assistant and the secretary were let go and Phil's wife, Dian, started working part-time at no pay and Phil and John took cuts in their salaries to slave wages. In 1974 and 1975 Phil and John worked 12 and 14 hours a day developing new applications for their computer software expertise. I was very encouraged one day in the midst of our problems when Phil said, "We are determined to make a business out of this dim situation come hell or high water." I had wondered many times before, but now knew that Phil was the entrepreneur who would make things happen.

Phil signed on a brokerage house to evaluate their portfolios and he signed on another bank to automate its Trust Department accounts. After further study it appeared that the small bank Trust Departments were an open invitation for computer software program contracts.

In the last six months of 1975 twelve banks were signed up for Trust Department automation. In addition, due to the dogged determination to succeed and the research and development effort and still other contracts, the partnership leaped into a substantial profit in December of 1975.

This venture has common traits with many if not most ventures. An early brush with success, then going broke, then responding to a burning desire to succeed. There are no silver platters in the market place. One gets what one earns with blood, sweat, tears, and second mortgages on homes, a wife pitching in to help without pay, and above all, the resolve to be a successful entrepreneur and make a viable business.

Recently I consolidated (the English call it amalgamated, the modern business word is conglomerated) all of the above and a few other investments into one new company called Capital Technology, Inc. Perhaps this will be the base for my encore in business. If I can make it grow, I might sell some stock.

The first venture undertaken by the new company was to publish this book. Publishers tell me that business books by unknown authors usually don't sell enough copies to break even, much less make a profit. I don't like profitless ventures, so I devised a strategy to make it profitable. I would wholesale the book by the dozens to a list of one hundred friends. The deal was an autographed copy, free, with the puchase of one dozen at a 20% discount—a baker's dozen for $96.

I had a hunch my friend, Ed Gaskins, at The American Bank would buy the deal, so I approached him first. He bought a dozen. Then, without revealing my first sale, I sold two other friends in the same bank a dozen each. The American Bank in Monroe is now well supplied with books.

Brother Oliver is a hard sell so I thought if I could sell him, I could go with confidence on down the list. He agreed, and since then I have sold sixty dozen and can pay for the publication. The others on my list of one hundred, not yet contacted, will be profitable.

The nice thing about this strategy is that the friends are not allowed to read the book before they buy it. I congratulate them as being "Patrons of the Arts." I have not yet contacted my art collector friend, Harry Dalton. He might buy two dozen.

Part VIII
RECAPITULATION

"History, it has often been observed, moves in a spiral; one returns to the preceding problem, but on a higher level, and by a corkscrew-like path. In this fashion we are going to return to entrepreneurship on a path that led out from a lower level, that of the single entrepreneur, to the manager, and now back, though upward, to entrepreneurship again." ... The Age of Discontinuity ... Peter F. Drucker

During my business activities I always liked to reserve a certain amount of time to "get my thinking done." To quote a very astute business friend of mine who had been on a treadmill of problems for several weeks:

"Jim, I've been so busy fighting fires lately that I've gotten way behind in my thinking."

When I became a pseudo-consultant for Teledyne in June 1970 I had the opposite kind of problem; i.e., too much time to think and too little action. It takes only so much time to read the daily paper, the *Wall Street Journal, Forbes, Fortune, Business Week, Barrons,* etc. Even with a new book every week or two there was still idle time. That is when I found idleness to be the devil's workshop and started reading old files and numerous business books and decided to write a book. That undertaking quickly turned into a full time job.

This part of the book incorporates some of my thinking and a recapitulation of the conglomerates, Teledyne, Allvac and other similar growth companies that have led me to a general procedure, not really a philosophy, for private investing. I hope it is a thoughtful, retrospective overview. You will see for yourself.

Chapter Thirty

HISTORICAL PERIODS OF INDUSTRY CONSOLIDATIONS

Before the recent decade of explosive industrial growth by acquisitive conglomerates there were two other periods of major industrial growth through the consolidation of companies, as illustrated in Figure 3. Each of the three periods had similar as well as different characteristics.

The first period occurred in the latter part of the 19th century and peaked in 1900 when 1200 companies disappeared through mergers.* It was characterized by the combining of competitive companies into major industrial monopolies. They were called "Trusts." The name, chosen by the business barons of that time, implied: "Trust the combines of competitive companies to monopolize whole segments of industry." But the government decided that such business combinations were not to be trusted and new laws declared them illegal.

The year 1879 marks the beginning of the period, with the organization of the Standard Oil Trust which combined 90% of the oil refining capacity in the United States. The years 1884 to 1887 saw the formation of the Cotton Seed Oil Trust, the Linseed Oil Trust, National Lead Trust, the Distillers and Cattle Feeders Trust, and the Sugar Trust. In 1889 the Diamond Match Company was formed and in 1890 the American Tobacco Company merged 162 firms to capture 90% of the market. In 1893 U. S. Rubber Company and General Electric Company were organized. U. S. Steel was formed between 1895 and 1904 with the combination of 170 firms and 65% of the market. Thousands of companies

---

*A detailed analysis of consolidation of companies is reported by Lynch in *Financial Performance of Conglomerates*. The statistics reported throughout this chapter are taken from that book and *Fortune* magazine, April 1973.

merged during this period to form a few dozen new industrial giants, each with monopolies in their marketplaces. Two of these companies (General Electric and U. S. Steel) are of particular interest to me. I was employed for a number of years by General Electric and I have been associated directly and indirectly with the steel industry, although I was never employed by U. S. Steel.

In 1900 General Electric had sales of $22,000,000, one half the sales of Allvac Metals last year, but in different dollars, of course. When I went to General Electric in 1937 its sales were $387,000,000, less than Teledyne's sales shortly after it merged with Vasco. Before I left General Electric its sales exceeded $1 billion and now are $14 billion—pretty good growth. Since those early days General Electric has continued to grow, not so much by continuing to acquire as by internal growth spurred by its renowned industrial research. It is now a Dow Jones "blue chip."

In 1952, when Paxton was president of General Electric, he bemoaned the fact that General Electric had grown primarily with the electrical industry market and couldn't improve on its 30% share of that market for years and years prior to that time. But General Electric has pioneered in markets outside the electrical industry—steam turbines, gas turbines, chemicals, nuclear energy, and many other areas. It is ironic, however, that General Electric, for the first time in its long history of technical innovations, gave up a major new technology when it threw in the sponge on the computer business and spun it off to Honeywell.

In contrast, U. S. Steel had a much stronger monopoly in steel than General Electric did in the electrical industry. That monopoly itself probably bred future stagnation and a reluctance by U. S. Steel to innovate the sponsor research. The monopoly was lost by their preoccupation with tonnage, controlling the mines, and resisting new technology. U. S. Steel followed the philosophy once enunciated by the great steel baron, Andrew Carnegie, who said, "Pioneers never make any money." So U. S. Steel didn't pioneer.

The market share enjoyed by U. S. Steel has steadily declined since 1905. General Electric, on the other hand, is renowned for forming the first major industrial research laboratory and supporting great scientists, inventors and

ACQUISITION OF MANUFACTURING AND MINING COMPANIES

1895 - 1972

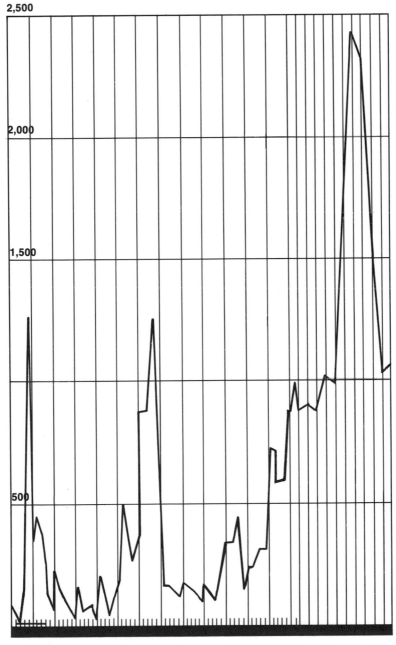

Fig. 3   *From Fortune Magazine*

engineers—Edison, Thomson, Steinmetz, Whitney and Coolidge. In 1935 a General Electric scientist, Langmuir, received the Nobel prize in chemistry. I doubt that U. S. Steel ever had a candidate for the Nobel prize, much less a winner. On the other hand, General Electric has not had a Nobel prize winner lately.

This first major period of mergers ended in 1903 with a business recession and a stock market crunch of 40%.

The second merger period occurred in the 1920s. It took a somewhat less monopolistic form in company consolidations, but in spite of the new laws against mergers for monopoly there seemed to be ways for smaller, second-class consolidation. This was the period when large utility holding companies were organized. Republic and Bethlehem, through acquisitions of smaller companies, became major competitors of U. S. Steel. Many of the mergers were designed to achieve vertical and horizontal integration and merchandising efficiency. This second period can be characterized by mergers of a wide variety of loosely related companies. As a result, the conglomerate type first appeared.

It was during the early part of that period that General Motors was formed. As pointed out by Lynch, a major contribution was made to the management theory and practice of large multi-division companies when Sloan of General Motors enunciated his organization theory for better management of large multi-division companies. Sloan advocated better measurement of results through decentralization and by the control and flow of capital to the cells of highest return.

Lynch suggests that this new form of General Motors organization influenced the shift to conglomerate type mergers because it enabled better control of widely diversified businesses.

About half of the companies formed during the past two major merger periods have thrived and grown. They now make up about one-half of the Dow Jones Industrial List of blue chips. The second period peaked in 1929 when 1245 companies disappeared through mergers. It died off in the thirties with the stock market crash and subsequent economic depression.

Chapter Thirty-One

TELEDYNE
IN THE DECADE
OF CONGLOMERATES

We come now to the acquisitive conglomerates and the third major period of mergers. This period began after World War II but moved slowly because of restrictive court rulings and new laws, until the conglomerate type companies began to flourish in the 60's. This period peaked in 1969 and then it subsided for the same reasons that caused the two earlier periods to subside: a business recession, a decline in earnings per share growth and a stock market crunch. Teledyne was formed in 1961, fairly early in the decade of the conglomerates.

The pattern of acquisitive conglomerates during the decade in which they flourished can be divided into three overlapping stages.

The first stage was led by Litton, the pioneer, in the late fifties and the first half of the sixties coincident with the formation of many other new conglomerate companies such as Teledyne. Some older companies such as ITT were transformed into conglomerates by the infusion of new and aggressive management. The creed was simple: grow fast in earnings per share by pooling acquisitions made by the exchange of the high multiple conglomerate stock for low multiple stock in the companies acquired. During the early stages the size of acquisitions tended to be relatively small and each tended to be a growth-oriented company. Pooling growth plus growth attracted go-go fund managers and brokers and the price/earnings ratio of conglomerates rose rapidly. The high multiple, in turn, supported the acceleration of the conglomerate acquisitions and on went the parade—an increase in earnings per share year after year.

The second stage began in the middle sixties. More and more acquisitive conglomerates appeared on the scene, acquisitions became more competitive, the companies for sale became more sophisticated, and their prices went up. The conglomerates grew to substantial sizes and in turn they had to make larger and larger acquisitions. The number of good companies available declined while the number of bad companies available increased. The net result was that growth began to slow down when larger, overpriced, non-growth companies were pooled. Therefore, earnings per share leveled off as the number of larger non-growing and even declining companies began to predominate the conglomeration of companies.

The third stage set in when the conglomerates began to pay still higher and higher multiples for larger and larger companies having less and less growth potential. Desperation came when the conglomerates began to guarantee the future prices of their stock to the acquired company. Earnings of some of the older, larger, more stolid companies declined with the beginning of a business recession. All combined, this resulted in less and less increase in earnings and the go-go fund managers and brokers began to dump the conglomerate stocks. Then the stock market decline in 1969 ended the conglomerate parade.

Teledyne's earnings per share continued to rise rapidly in 1966, '67 and '68. The price earnings multiple continued at a lofty level and in a strong bull market the price of Teledyne soared. Teledyne had acquired well over one hundred companies—I'd estimate 150 total—and was continuing to acquire at a rapid pace. During this time each deal continued to result in an immediate increase in Teledyne earnings per share. For example, at one point when Teledyne earnings were $1 per share and the stock price was $60 (60 x E), we acquired companies whose earnings were also $1 per share but paid a price of only $10 per share (10 x E). This followed the conglomerate creed—increase earnings per share by acquiring low multiple stocks with Teledyne's high multiple stock. The parade galloped on, but nothing lasts forever.

Some of the companies acquired for 10 x E appeared to be attractive at the time but in many cases they had a mundane future, which was precisely the reason that they were cheap in the marketplace. For example, during this period I bought an iron foundry for Teledyne at 10 x E. I certainly had mixed emotions about its future promise even though it did have excellent management who knew how to make a profit in that difficult industry.

Some time ago, just after we merged with Teledyne, I asked Arthur Rock, a director of Teledyne and a prominent venture capital investor in San Francisco, "How long and how fast can a company grow?" He commented:

"I have thought about that many times. I have observed the Litton situation. By an active acquisition program with a high multiple stock, Litton has been able to grow successfully in a decade to $2 billion in sales and has consistently increased earnings per share. Size is apparently not a limiting factor."

Litton's earnings peaked in 1967 at $2.54 per share. Then in 1969 its long unbroken record of growth for a dozen years ended when earnings declined to $1.78 per share. Deficits appeared in 1972. Roy Ash, the "Wonder Boy" president, went to Nixon's staff to manage the Federal budget.

The price earnings multiple on Litton stock dropped from the lofty level of 60 to less than 10. The stock price fell from $120 per share in 1967, to $60 per share in 1968, and to $15 per share in 1970, but even that was not final; the price fell to $10 in 1972.

The demise of Litton's growth resulted in a massive public re-evaluation of conglomerate stock prices and Teledyne was not immune. The price of Teledyne stock faltered when its earnings growth rate slowed down in '68 and '69 and the price collapsed when flat earnings were reported in 1970. It was pushed still further down concomitant with the bad stock market climate. Conglomerate stocks, which had been the market sweethearts in the early sixties, changed to market outcasts.

In the latter six months of 1969, the Teledyne stock price declined from a high of $70 to a low of $13 per share. The formula that had worked so well for a decade had ended. Perhaps real values were coming home to roost but a billion dollar company had grown up overnight.

Teledyne didn't grow as fast after it acquired Vasco, its first major acquisition and the first large one that subsequently caused the negative effect on earnings per share.

As pointed out before, Vasco at that time was profitable and had an excellent balance sheet, and Henry Singleton bought it cheap with Teledyne's inflated priced shares. The pooled result was an immediate big gain in Teledyne earnings per share.

When Vasco was acquired it consisted of eight cells (units or divisions). It is of interest to look at what subsequently happened to each of those Vasco cells. The first constructive action taken by Teledyne was to separate each of the divisions into separate profit centers. That spotlight alone separated the cells as follows:

MEFCO, a metal forming job shop in Indiana, had been acquired by Vasco some years before from its founding entrepreneur, Sims. Sims retired shortly thereafter, as most entrepreneurs do when they sell out. The late Tom Collins took over. He was an excellent caretaker. For five years MEFCO was bled, no new capital was invested, the old line products faded, but during this period, as often happens with a completely depreciated plant, MEFCO's profits were excellent. When Vasco merged with Teledyne, Collins retired and the struggle began to rejuvenate the job shop with a new manager, Archie Spratt. New capital was invested and new product development was undertaken, and profits declined accordingly. Therefore, this cell of Vasco, now Teledyne, has not been a growth division but a unit that was bled by Vasco and is now a Teledyne loser.

Moving east, look at another Vasco cell, Armetco at Wooster, Ohio, formed by an entrepreneur, Ted Franks, and sold to Vasco in 1964 at the peak of its earnings record. Ted Franks got rich and relaxed when he sold out and the profits from Armetco were never again as good. In fact, it was closed down in 1967 after a miserable year of losses. The inevitable conclusion is that Armetco was a loser. It was liquidated.

Next consider the Colonial division acquired by Vasco in the 1930s and located in Monaca, Pennsylvania, on the Allegheny River north of Pittsburgh. Colonial and the Vasco parent company in Latrobe were duplications of each other. Colonial was operated on a cost basis as a fabricator for Vasco products and its value added was never properly accounted for in Vasco sales. It was never very profitable and certainly not a growth cell in Teledyne.

Pittsburgh Tool Steel Wire was also located in the smoggy climate of Monaca by the river. PTSW was run by a savvy Dutchman, Henry Wimmersburger, the gentleman who took over as president of Vasco after it was acquired by Teledyne. Henry Wimmersburger continued to say grace over PTSW, and as a cell of Teledyne it continued to turn in an excellent profit. In fact, for a number of years PTSW had accounted for a very high percentage of Vasco's profits. It was in a special profitable niche of the industry producing special wire shapes. However, its growth potential was limited and earnings rose and fell with the cyclic steel industry. Again, PTSW was not a growth company for Teledyne.

The next cell is Vasco-Canada, a very small steel warehouse which was kept afloat by transferring steel from the Vasco plant at cost or less. Vasco-Canada had been a loser for years until the name was changed to Teledyne-Canada and it was used effectively as a corporate shell for making a number of profitable acquisitions in Canada. The original Vasco-Canada cell contributed nothing to Teledyne but losses and a continuation of inventory write-offs.

Another small division of Vasco, Nem Labs in Cambridge, acquired from the professor-entrepreneur Nick Grant, was liquidated.

Vasco, the parent cell in the complex, had a long history of slow and ponderous growth but was now a satisfied and lazy company.

The original Vasco cell was only modestly profitable and certainly not growing. The combined profits of all the cells at the time of the acquisition were good but erratic and cyclic.

The departure of managers at Vasco has been very detrimental to its progress in the past few years. The Vasco managers have come and gone in rapid succession. All of the Vasco vice presidents who were there at the time of the merger soon departed. Second, the overhead at the Vasco parent plant was never trimmed to size when Teledyne separated the other profit centers. Third, the capital invested by Teledyne has probably been one-fifth of that invested by Vasco's nearest competitors, and that was too much. Much of the capital that has been invested has been a debacle. Therefore, Vasco, the parent cell, is not a growth company but wanders slightly up and far down in the cyclic steel industry. It was very sick in 1970 to 1972.

Allvac was part of Vasco for less than a year. Therefore, it was never really combined but continued as a separate Teledyne profit center. As a separate company, it is the only company of the Vasco cells that has since continued to thrive in sales and profit growth. What has happened to Allvac since merging is more fully reviewed in a later chapter.

Admittedly, the above is a generalized review since the Teledyne merger, but it is sufficient to categorize each cell as either plus or minus in profit growth contribution to Teledyne.

Growth	Cyclic Earnings	Declining in Earnings
Allvac		Nem Lab—liquidated
	PTSW	Vasco Canada—loser
	Vasco parent	MEFCO—bled
	Colonial	Armetco—liquidated

This negative effect set in very shortly after Teledyne acquired Vasco. This would seem to support my thesis that the acquisition of Vasco was the first major mistake that Teledyne made. One growth company, plus three cyclic so-so companies, plus four negative companies add up, at least, to a temporary decline in earnings per share. This sample can be viewed in another way. Think of each of these divisions as venture investment. Allvac has turned into a sales and earnings growth "bonanza" in the subsequent eight years and more than compensated for the poor apples. So, in time, Teledyne has practiced liquidation of the losers and further investment for growth of the bonanza—Allvac. The longer range result might be positive.

I wonder if the sample extends to Teledyne as a whole? If it does, we would divide Teledyne's 150-odd companies as follows: 20 growth cells, 60 cyclic cells, 80 declining cells. Of course the Teledyne insurance companies represent several of the growth cells and no doubt make up for a lot of the laggards. In 1975, however, millions in losses were written off when Augonot Insurance Company fell into the medical liability hole.

Some specific information on Teledyne cells was made public by Roberts at the Teledyne annual meeting in March of 1973. He reported on 130 profit centers, twenty less than the 150 a few years ago, which indicates that about 20 have either been liquidated or merged with others during the past three years. He also reported that 34 of the 130 chalked up record profits in 1972. George stated this case in that positive way, as you would expect him to do, citing the 34 good ones. I would put the case in the opposite context by saying that almost 100 Teledyne cells did not grow in 1972. The 34 that did grow is more than my guesstimation of 20, but 1972 was a banner business year and my guesstimate of 20 for the average of the last three years is probably about right. Allvac Metals was cited by Roberts as one of the prominent growth companies. I should add that Wah Chang has also been a star.

Teledyne earnings peaked at $2.00 in 1969 and have since drifted lower. But Singleton is a determined man and still has the insatiable appetite to increase earnings per share. His latest fling was to buy 25% of Teledyne's outstanding shares and flip the first reported quarter of 1972 from 41c to 55c per share. He again reports growth of this sort.

Teledyne grew from $1 million in sales in 1961 to more than $1.3 billion in 1971. I suspect this growth was too fast to be properly managed and many of the founders of the companies departed and untried managers were broken in to replace them.

To keep a lid on this proliferation Teledyne unsuccessfully tried to practice management retention. The 150-odd companies acquired by Teledyne each had a hard-headed boss man running it and frequently he was also the owner or an entrepreneur. That man typically had the entrepreneurial flair—the pleasure of being his own boss. Then, immediately after merging, he was confronted with the frustrations of adjusting himself to bean counters and to being directed by new bosses and unfamiliar systems.

It was inevitable that the entrepreneurs grew restless

and began to leave. They couldn't make the transition from being their own boss to being bossed, but also management retention problems were compounded. The older mature companies acquired tended to be managed by presidents who were older and mature. Having reached their highest leval of incompetence, they had learned to relax in the pleasure of quiet stockholders and mediocre profits and routine operations without disturbing the peace with innovations. The presidents of the older companies, not unlike the entrepreneurs, found themselves in a new and foreign environment. They felt they were under the control of a new conglomerate not yet dry behind the ears, with no organizational cohesion, without a scrap of written policy, yet dispatching from their corporate office bean counters and lawyers and group executives. I was one of those, too. The older men sought to secure themselves a "chairman" and await early retirement. The net result was the loss of both the young and the old. In turn the major reorganization of the conglomerate companies has set in and will continue for years.

However, one of the young Teledyne managers told me recently that Teledyne will be a better company when it finally purges itself of the old timers and fills its management group with ambitious young professional managers. Whether right or wrong, that very change in the character of management has rapidly occurred in the past two or three years. But it takes time to fit young professionals to companies which have tended to be one-man operations. Consequently, for the past two or three years earnings per share have flattened and recently declined. This transition from entrepreneurial management of individual companies to the professional management of the divisions in the conglomerate will take still longer before the present growth stagnation can be arrested and hopefully future growth from within will commence. I was directly involved in this period when the entrepreneurs were leaving; in fact, I was one that left. Professional managers who replaced them seemed to have a success probability of less than 50-50; i.e., two have to be tried to find one. This process takes time and saps earnings. Such management discombobulation in dozens and dozens of divisions of a billion dollar company will take a long time to stabilize. The company as a whole must mature. Following that, earnings per share might grow again.

Thirty or forty years from now, businessmen will look back on the decade of the conglomerates between 1960 and 1970 and assess it. Perhaps then Teledyne will be considered one of the great companies formed during that period—a General Motors or General Electric. In the 1960s Teledyne did lead *Fortune*'s list of 500 industries in average annual growth rate in both net income and in earnings per share. It was second in sales growth rate with a 63.5 compounded annual growth in earnings per share for ten years. It is hard to imagine that this will be matched by any company for years and years to come.

Chapter Thirty-Two

GROWTH COMPANY PATTERNS

New companies and growth companies appear on the market scene like waves flowing from the sea and some regularly disappear like the tides going out. For any company to maintain a steep growth rate is a formidable management task and very few accomplish it for a prolonged period of time.

Investing venture capital in new companies is by definition venturesome—gains can be substantial, so can losses. Even when the combination of the entrepreneur and the product idea are initially judged to be excellent the investor is lucky if one in ten ventures turns into a bonanza or a ten- to twenty-fold gain. Some will surely fail, some will be just so-so, but one bonanza in ten can more than compensate for the failures. This kind of investing takes patience. The right company is hard to find.

A good system for spotlighting the new growth companies as they flow on the scene should be possible because those have some earnings growth histories to evaluate. There are always new companies lurking in the over-the-counter market which are "comers"—new IBM's, Polaroid and Xeroxs—and there should be a systematic way to find them and invest early, before they mature and before they are publicly recognized and finally overpriced. A good system must sound the alarm to sell out before the tide of growth in earnings subsides and their price skids from lofty levels to the basement.

In a search for investing strategies it is pertinent to re-examine the wide fluctuations in the prices of Allvac and Teledyne stocks. This will enable us to relate the variations to the fundamental earning growth performances of the companies and relate the influence of the market climate to stock price during the era of the sixties.

Both Allvac and Teledyne are examples of companies that were founded with an idea and initially backed with venture capital. Allvac, of course, was relatively a small potato. Both temporarily became growth companies and each passed through extremely wide fluctuations in public value. The two companies are good illustrations within my past experience of my interest in venture capital and growth company investments.

As illustrated in Figure 4, one dollar of venture capital initially invested in Allvac was worth $14 (30 x E) three to four years later. Allvac, after two teething years, had three years of rapidly rising earnings per share and then was classified in the stock market as a growth company. When growth in earnings faltered, Allvac by definition ceased to be a growth company—a sell signal for shrewd investors— the price per share dropped to $3.50, 10 x E.

Teledyne grew at a very steep compounded rate for eight years and its stock price skyrocketed. The Teledyne price earnings multiple peaked at 70 x E, coincident with its steepest growth period and the price peaked at $72 per share, but when sales and the earnings growth slowed down and other adverse circumstances came together to end the exalted public expectations for conglomerates, the price dropped to $13 per share, 7 x E. When earnings growth slowed down, Teledyne was delisted as a growth company. The sellers flooded in and the buyers left town.

The A, B, Cs of the price life cycle of growth companies as experienced in both Allvac and Teledyne can be generalized to fit most growth companies. Earnings per share is the basic reason for the price fluctuations. Figure 4 typifies the principle for growth companies. The complete cycle can be divided into three parts; (A) birth, (B) growth, and (C) maturity.

(A) The newly born venture capital company has its stock initially traded over-the-counter. During the teething period, with no earnings history, the price per share drifts up and down in some relation to the investor's hope or expectations for future earnings. Occasionally the price will rise to an absurd figure if the business is exciting and glamorous like "computers" and "environmental," but for the less glamorous new company the price usually remains close to the issue price. It is subject to supply and demand and general market conditions while the public waits for

STOCK PRICES FOR ALLVAC, VASCO & TELEDYNE

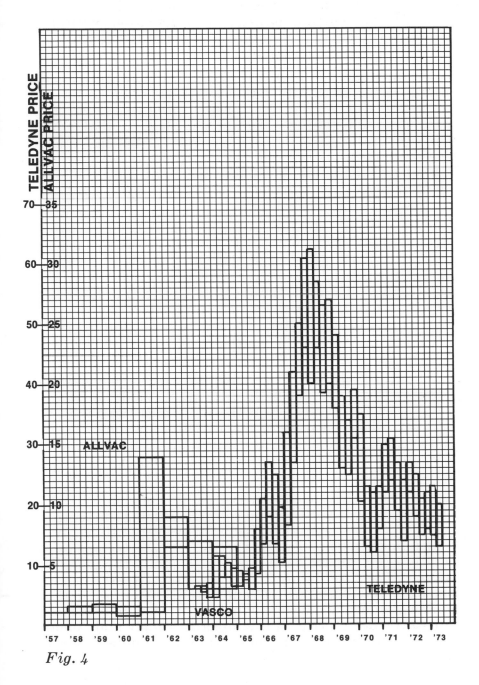

Fig. 4

profits. If the teething period goes beyond two to three years the investor tires of waiting and the stock price tends to sag—it is a so-so company. If losses continue too long and the venture can go "belly up," the price drops to nothing.

In many cases the venture capital company spends all its money before it is profitable, as Allvac did, and refinancing is necessary.

In this example, Allvac and Teledyne succeeded and earnings per share rose and the companies entered the growth period (B). The stock price shifted from one based on only hope to a new scale based on the earnings growth record. If earnings rise fast, the price rises fast and the P/E ratio rises from 10 to 20 to 30 x E, as Allvac's did for three years before earnings faltered. If steep growth continues for five or six years, as Teledyne's did, the P/E will rise absurdly high, to 70 or more.

The stock price fluctuates in some relation to the market as a whole, higher when the market is bullish and lower when bearish.

The actual P/E multiple will also vary significantly with the type of business. Levitz, a unique marketer of furniture with a steep and lengthening growth record, reached a P/E multiple of 100 in a strong market, whereas Southern Railroad, in spite of a good four years growth record, is a stolid company because it is a railroad and its multiple hasn't risen above 10 x E. The average for the Dow stocks was 17 x E when the Dow Jones industrial averages passed 1,000 late in '72.

But nothing grows forever. Maturity some day is inevitable (C). When growth slows down, the stock price levels off and the P/E drops and when growth in earnings declines the stock price collapses to levels as low or lower than the Dow companies' average of 17 x E. The company matures and enters a period where maintenance of earnings is a future problem. If earnings are up, the price of the stock moves slowly up; if down, the price slides down and thereafter remains within a low P/E ratio of 15 ± 10, typical of the mature and ponderous company. Earnings are no longer moving steadily and steeply upward year after year. If this trend is slightly upward but erratic over the years, such as

General Electric's has been over a long history, then the multiple will creep up again, perhaps to 20 x E in a bull market. Now the company is a "blue chip," which means big and old but with a lengthening history of long term slow growth. The historical characteristics of a company's earnings are the bedrock factor in setting the public price of its stock in relationship with others. None are immune to the ups and downs of bear and bull markets. Of course, brokers on their telephones are always turning up fads but they usually fade away to real value in a short time.

Part IX
EPILOGUE

Chapter Thirty-Three

TELEDYNE LATELY

It has been five years since I have been closely associated with the affairs of Teledyne. My interest in that glamorous company has continued and I read about it in the papers and talk with friends still employed there.

Teledyne's steep growth in earnings tapered off in 1969 and peaked in 1970, and with a depressed stock market the price of Teledyne shares fell precipitously. Consequently, Teledyne's rapid growth by acquisitions died off.

Remember, during the hey-day of acquisitions, we bought dozens of companies at a price/earnings ratio of 10 to 20. So when Teledyne multiple fell below 10 in 1970, 1971 and 1972, Singleton devised a new strategy. He decided that Teledyne should buy Teledyne, the best bargain around. Several favorable financial conditions enabled Teledyne to launch a massive stock repossession plan: 1) Small companies that were losers, such as examples cited in Chapter 38, as well as some major losers such as Packard Bell, were liquidated. 2) Growth companies, estimated at 30% of all Teledyne Companies, grew rapidly in profits. 3) Favorable cash built up from depreciation and modest profits from Teledyne's "asset companies." 4) No cash dividends were paid out. 5) A stringent tightening of corporate cash management was introduced. 6) Rigid controls were set up on the investments of new capital. All in all, from a financial point of view, Teledyne was extremely well managed and the bankers, therefore, smiled and agreed to loan Teledyne millions of dollars on their untapped borrowing power. Teledyne put all these things together and launched their massive stock repurchase plan in 1972.

Through six tender offers, from 1972 to early 1976, Teledyne re-acquired 22.3 million of the outstanding shares at an average price of $21.50 per share. This, with other conversions, reduced the total outstanding shares from 36 million to about 12 million and raised the debt equity ratio to about 1 to 1.

The effect of all this is almost unbelievable. The 70%

reduction in outstanding shares increased materially the pro-rata ownership of the remaining shareholders who held on and stuck with it through thick and thin. The dramatic effect is illustrated by the following examples:

Singleton's ownership in Teledyne was increased from about 2% to about 6%. His pro-rata share of the $100,000,000 earned in 1975, would be about $6,000,000. That is a 27 fold annual gain on his $225,000 original investment to start Teledyne. His $350,000 salary fades in comparison to a meaningless figure.

The effect of the stock repurchase on the old Vasco stockholders that held on is a classic story, too. Taking stock dividends into account, the present 12,000,000 shares outstanding is very near the number of shares outstanding after Teledyne acquired Vasco in 1966. At that time, Vasco owners held a 20% interest in Teledyne. If they had all held their interest, they would have gone through a dilution in that interest to about 7%, when 36 million shares were out. But then as a result of the repossession plan, Teledyne's outstanding shares fell from 36 million to 12 million and in turn the old Vasco stockholders' pro-rata interest rose again back to 20%. Vasco's pro-rata interest of 20% of the 1975 $100,000,000 earnings would be $20,000,000. This figure compares with only $3.5 million earned by Vasco the year before it merged with Teledyne. This figure, $20,000,000, is 2/3 of the 1966 $30,000,000 in total Vasco stockholders equity, a 66% annual return on the old Vasco stockholders equity. I don't know of any of Vasco's sister stoic steel companies that have fared so well in such a short time.

Another example relates to my favorite company— Allvac Metals. Allvac shareholders held a 13% interest in Vasco after the two merged in 1965. Therefore, the Allvac shareholders (assuming all held on) would now have a 13% interest in Vasco pro-rata interest of $20 million, or, $2.6 million. Allvac earned only 1/4 million dollars the year before it merged with Vasco and Allvac's stockholders equity then was only $826,000. The kind people who invested $1.00 for one share in Allvac would now, March 1976, have 1/2 of a Teledyne share with a market value of about $25, and a pro-rata interest in Teledyne earnings of $4.00 annually/ share.

The final example gets down to me personally. My maximum ownership in Allvac was 80,000 shares, so if I had held on through thick and thin, pro-rata interest would be $320,000 annually. But I didn't, so "that milk got spilt."

My hat is off to Sir Singleton and his singular success in fashioning Teledyne into a 2 billion dollar industrial empire in fifteen eventful years. First, he practiced a massive outpour of Teledyne shares to acquire other companies. Then he practiced a massive repossession and gathered in 70% of these shares so recently passed out. Using as collateral the profits and the balance sheets from those recently acquired companies seems a little like financial legerdemain.

Teledyne, in fifteen short years, has reached sales of $2 billion. It took G. E. almost sixty years to grow to $2 billion. Then it achieved $14 billion sales in the next twenty years. Do you suppose Teledyne will reach $14 billion in the next two decades?

If that can be done without issuing more shares, then sales would be $1000 per share and profits might be $50. per share, equal to the present price.

During the past three years I have been playing with Teledyne's tender offers, i.e., buying Teledyne stock quickly after a tender offer and then tendering the stock at a higher price, thus making a profit. I should reinvest some of that profit in Teledyne stock before Singleton surprises us again and shows earnings of $10.00 per share in 1976.

Today is April 1, 1976 (April Fool's Day), and I just finished dialing my broker and bought 500 shares of Teledyne at the same price I sold some for seven years ago. But when I sold, earnings were $1.50 a share. Those shares I just bought cost $50 7/8 per share. That price, at $10.00 earnings, would be a P/E multiple of 5 X E. This happens to be consistent with my recent strategy to buy low multiple stocks in high class companies.

The following graph, No. 5, shows the gyrations of Allvac and Teledyne stock prices through the first quarter of 1976. I am frequently asked what the future price of Teledyne will be and I respond with a consistent and accurate answer "The future price will fluctuate."

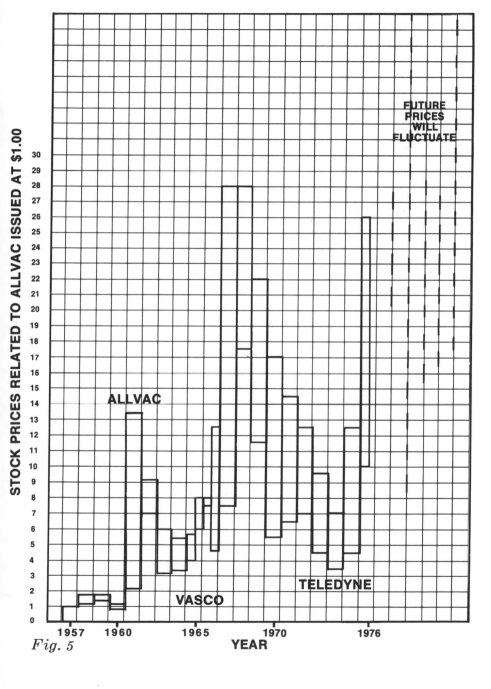

ALLVAC, VASCO
AND TELEDYNE
STOCK PRICES

STOCK PRICES RELATED TO ALLVAC ISSUED AT $1.00

FUTURE
PRICES
WILL
FLUCTUATE

ALLVAC

VASCO

TELEDYNE

Fig. 5

YEAR

1957   1960   1965   1970   1976

213

Chapter Thirty-Four

WAH CHANG REVISITED

This is a recent sequel in the tale of Wah Chang. My daughter, Mary, graduated from the University of Oregon in December 1974. She liked Oregon and stayed on without a supporting job. She knew from my earlier admonition to Jim and Jack that once a graduate, she was on her own. I sent Mary $1,000 for a graduation present knowing she was very unsettled in her jobs of "dog washing" and "bus driving." Mary came home in April of 1975 for two weeks and we had a delightful vacation with her. We had a couple of walks together at Aero Plantation. During the walks we chatted lightly and seriously about Mary's plans for her future. Mary was obviously searching for a plan for her life and livelihood. Her interest was in dogs and horses, but she had economic problems in living in that realm. I suggested to her that she contact Steve Yih of Teledyne Wah Chang at Albany—30 or 40 miles from the University of Oregon. She said, "No, I don't like that idea." I told her that her mother, Kay, had worked as a lab technician in chemistry when I met her in Indiana thirty years ago. She had worked as a technician because she was an ambitious chemistry student. She wanted to graduate cum laude in chemistry.

Mary said, "What's the big deal about cum laude?"

I said, "Nothing, Mary, nothing. Look at a job as a living and to hell with cum laude."

Mary said, "I only want a kennel of dogs or a stable of horses—understand, dad?"

I replied, "Yes, Mary, I understand."

Mary returned to Eugene with $50 and called a month later with $10 left. I told her again to see Yih at Wah Chang and get a job as a receptionist or a lab technician.

Mary had met Yih and his wife, May, when they visited with me a few times in North Carolina and she had had dinner with them at their home in Albany while she attended the University of Oregon.

In June, 1975, Mary reluctantly applied to Steve Yih for a job at Wah Chang and signed on as a lab technician there. Shortly afterward I called Steve and thanked him for hiring Mary. In the course of the conversation Steve seemed more than normally perturbed with his relationship with the Teledyne corporate office.

A few weeks later Mary called me and said, "Dad, there are rumors all over out here that a 'big management shakeup' is in the wind. What does that mean? Will Yih be affected?"

I responded to Mary, "I doubt it. Steve Yih is 'king of zirconium' so it seems doubtful to me that he would be affected."

For eight years, since the Teledyne classic acquisition of Wah Chang, it had continued to grow and profit under the shrewd and infallible management of Yih. I'd guess that Wah Chang in eight years must have delivered $40 to $50 million dollars cash to the Avenue of the Stars in Los Angeles. However, Yih, like my brother Oliver, lately had had troubles meshing with the gears at Teledyne's corporate headquarters in Los Angeles.

On Friday, September 5, 1975, the following headline appeared in the Albany *Oregonian:*

"LONG TIME WAH CHANG LEADER AXED."

Yih's pride was no doubt mortally wounded. After all, Yih had built a world renowned company in the field of exotic metals and Yih, himself, was well recognized around the world as "king of zirconium." I understand that Fred Kauffman, Vice President of Teledyne, unexpectedly appeared on the scene at Albany and announced a take-over, like a Latin American coup. He installed a retired admiral recently hired by Roberts and/or Singleton as the new president of Wah Chang.

I called Steve to express my regrets.

"What now, Steve?" I asked.

He said, "The big doctor offered me a job in the far eastern division at Hong Kong."

"Oh—Teledyne's Siberia, eh?"

Steve responded, "A place for me to go and rot."

Some years before, when I was temporarily managing Wah Chang, Steve said to me, "We had better get long-term contracts with Teledyne and at the end when we are finished they might give us a gold watch."

So I asked Steve, "Did you get the gold watch?"

Steve said, "No."

Steve went to Hong Kong for a few weeks and returned to have a final confrontation with Singleton. Then he left Teledyne employment and set out to finance and organize his own company to produce zirconium in competition with Wah Chang. Singleton took a calculated risk in axing Yih, and didn't realize he was also outraging Yih's loyal managers in that plant. Several of twenty loyal "Yihites" have already left Wah Chang and joined Steve in his new enterprise. I hear Yih has financial backing, and the Chinese tong commences again, eight years since peace was made with Teledyne. One by one the capable technicians and managers of Wah Chang will depart to Yih's new company. It will be interesting to see how Yih fares as the entrepreneur building his own zirconium plant. It will be equally as interesting to see how Wah Chang fares without its management.

Chapter Thirty-Five
FINALLY ALLVAC METALS

I really don't know much about those non-material companies in Teledyne's host of companies such as Packard Bell (I believe it was liquidated), or Augonot Insurance (I believe I read some place they wrote off $80,000,000 to cover doctors' liability claim problems), nor Waterpik, which I hear is doing well, or those several dozens of other Teledyne companies. I do know in the material group of Teledyne companies that Wah Chang and Allvac have been the star performers.

Allvac is one of the greatest cells in the honeycomb of Teledyne companies. I have been divorced from direct Allvac management for ten years and from Teledyne management for five years; therefore, my vantage point is, as you can expect, most definitely objective with malice toward none.

After I relinquished my direct management of Allvac when it was merged with Teledyne in 1965, Ted Franks became president for a short time. When Teledyne Titanium was organized Franks reluctantly assumed responsibility for it for about a year before he retired and Oliver Nisbet became head of Allvac and Teledyne Titanium.

Now, galloping ahead four years, Buddy Vaughn is heading up Teledyne Titanium and John Andrews is the chief at Allvac. Oliver continued as the nervous group executive, wondering when George Roberts might insert someone from the steel industry as another layer of management between Teledyne Corporate and the Allvac and Titanium companies.

Buddy Vaughn, a very smart engineer and gregarious salesman, did a phenomenal job, with capable assistants like Johnny Pigg and Dave Sims, of holding Teledyne Titanium profitable in a terrible climate. The teething period lasted a rather long time and Teledyne Titanium survived in the rough titanium business.

John Andrews, as head of Allvac, fashioned that company into one of the largest and the most profitable of the super alloy producers in the metals industry. Under Oliver's value-of-the-dollar tutelage, this dogged and determined but brilliant man made Allvac better than all those competitors who at one time purchased metal from Allvac and who also sought to merge with Allvac, the pioneer in super alloys.

Allvac and Teledyne Titanium are now doing an annual business of about $40 million, about the same as the sales of Vasco metals when we merged with it, and its net profits are about $2 million annually.

Oliver Nisbet managed both Allvac and Teledyne Titanium from 1970 to the middle of 1975. As a Teledyne executive over these two Monroe, North Carolina, companies, Oliver got increasingly crossed up with the corporate office. Oliver is a very independent thinker and when he makes up his mind he is like the Rock of Gibraltar and very difficult to change. He is particularly difficult to change after he has thought long and hard about a major capital outlay such as a $5 million forging press. That is naturally a big bite for Teledyne when they study their flow of capital to alternative electronic company needs and calculate comparative rates of return. Oliver is also a little too independent to mesh smoothly with the inevitable confinement and restrictions of a large company. His relationship with the big bosses, particularly Singleton, deteriorated and festered. Then in June 1975, Fred Kauffman, the Teledyne Vice President, appeared in Monroe and took over, making John Andrews President of both Allvac and Teledyne Titanium. George Roberts is reported to have said, "I didn't fire Oliver." Oliver told me, "I didn't resign, Jim."

While Oliver reigned over the Monroe companies I'd estimate he delivered $15 million to the corporate treasury on The Avenue of the Stars in Los Angeles. It would have been nice if that money could have resided in the American Bank & Trust Company in Monroe rather than the Bank of America in Los Angeles. That idea brings up many alternative notions that can be retroacted.

Roberts and Singleton certainly fulfilled the basic deal I made with them when we merged; i.e., they would provide the necessary capital, and it has been millions of dollars, to match and fulfill the business opportunities which abounded at Allvac. That they did, sometimes reluctantly, but that they did. Whether or not that much money could have been generated from the profits and whether or not the local banks would have helped is an academic question, but it's doubtful. Perhaps more Allvac stock could have been sold to grow on, but I chose not to pursue that course.

I have no regrets, but my conclusion is firm: Good growth companies like Allvac should not associate with stale companies like Vasco nor with companies like Teledyne which buy stale companies and stagnate in the conglomeration of good and bad. Ellis, in his book, *Institutional Investor*, calls such business "cross sterilization." Advice to fellow entrepreneurs: Don't merge growth companies—do merge stale companies. But know when to get out.

Allvac goes on. Why? (1) The people running Allvac now are pretty much the same people except the two old Nisbets. (2) They have a high sense of responsibility and integrity and ability. (3) They are young, ambitious, and energetic. (4) They were instilled with business integrity by the founder. (5) They are uninhibited by the stoic influences of the steel industry. (6) The company has not until recently been cluttered up by tiers of hierarchy between the local management and the president of Teledyne.

A couple of years ago I met a lady in Monroe who told me she had invested $800 in Allvac in 1961. Since that time she has gotten Vasco stock and now has Teledyne stock with only half as many shares and the value is less than $800. She has received no dividends except stock. She thinks zero growth in a span of ten years is nothing to write home about. I agreed, but then she asked me a tough question: "Why did you merge that nice little company with those steel fellows in Pittsburgh called Vasco, and then with those electronic fellows in California called Teledyne, and how can they boss it and continue to nurture its growth as well as you did without them?"

I didn't answer her. It was late in the afternoon and I walked away toward the sunset.